If Mama Goes South, We're All Going with Her

Other books by Lindsey O'Connor

If Mama Ain't Happy, Ain't Nobody Happy
Moms Who Changed the World
The Christian's Guide to Working From Home
Working at Home

For more information about Lindsey's other books or to contact her, visit her web site at Lindseyo.com.

If you would like to book Lindsey O'Connor for a speaking engagement, contact:

Speak Up Speaker Services
810-982-0898 or toll-free 888-870-7719
speakupinc@aol.com
www.speakupspeakerservices.com

If Mama
Goes South,
We're All
Going with Her

Lindsey O'Connor

Fleming H. Revell
A Division of Baker Book House Co
Grand Rapids, Michigan 49516

Published by Fleming H. Revell
a division of Baker Book House Company
P.O. Box 6287, Grand Rapids, MI 49516-6287
www.bakerbooks.com

Printed in the United States of America

Library of Congress Cataloging-in-Publication Data is on file at the Library of Congress, Washington, D.C.

ISBN 0-8007-5797-1

Unless otherwise indicated, Scripture is taken from the NEW AMERICAN STANDARD BIBLE ®. Copyright © The Lockman Foundation 1960, 1962, 1963, 1968, 1971, 1972, 1973, 1975, 1977, 1995. Used by permission.

Scripture marked MESSAGE is taken from THE MESSAGE. Copyright © by Eugene H. Peterson 1993, 1994, 1995. Used by permission of NavPress Publishing Group.

Scripture marked NIV is taken from the HOLY BIBLE, NEW INTERNA-TIONAL VERSION®. NIV®. Copyright © 1973, 1978, 1984 by International Bible Society. Used by permission of Zondervan. All rights reserved.

To Timothy

Contents

Foreword

"Becky, I have a favor to ask you." The voice on the other end of the phone was that of my dear, very pregnant friend, Lindsey O'Connor.

"Anything!" I offered. Who can deny a friend any request in her ninth month?

"I know you're house-sitting here in Colorado Springs this week, to get away and work on a deadline. Right?"

"Yes," I replied, "Vicki Caruana offered her home for a writing haven, and boy, do I need it. It's Texas. It's August. Her house is near the mountains. Need I say more?"

"Oh, Becky," Lindsey sighed. "I have bad news for you. Texas heat has moved to Colorado. I'm sweltering here. Is there any chance Vicki has air conditioning?"

"Not only that," I replied, a smile of realization crossing my face. "But she has a spare bedroom, a sun porch, and promises to leave plenty of Starbucks coffee and chocolate. You want to stay with me for a week and relax and write?"

"That would be a dream!" Lindsey said. "Tim is actually the one who suggested it, knowing I needed to finish this book and that I might go south before it gets written if I don't have a break—and a little cool air on my swollen, overheated body."

"Come on, girlfriend!" I encouraged her. "Let's do it."

And thus began one of the most idyllic weeks of writing and friendship that I've ever enjoyed. In fact, I've never spent an entire week alone with a writing friend—focusing only on writing, prayer, soul-sharing, and eating out, and all done at a leisurely pace. It was a true oasis of the heart for both of us in a year that had just about "done us in." I was reminded of the week Anne Morrow Lindbergh (wife of the famous aviator, Charles Lindbergh) spent at a beach house with her sister, away from husband, kids, phone, and demands. They'd visit and share breakfast in the morning, take lingering walks along the ocean's shore, then close the doors as they each tended to their own projects during the day, uninter-rupted—a luxury in and of itself. Then as evening drew near, they'd gather to share the day's writing produce, along with a simple meal. The result of that week was *A Gift from the Sea,* a classic book for women about simplicity and slowing down to the heartbeat of life.

Our week together allowed Lindsey the space and comfort to finish writing this nourishing, heart-tending book for women, her gift from the mountains to you. She began the project with small bits of time caught between homeschooling, overseeing the building and decorating of her new home, baking cakes (from scratch!), walking in the country, and loving her husband and children and friends. Even at nine months pregnant and in terrible back pain, Lindsey looked serene and lovely.

I do not know how she pulled it off.

There were many times, as you will see in these pages, that she wondered about this as well. And it was during that wondering when she began to seek an even deeper life and ask the Lord what he really required of her. Was she doing too much? What could she let go of? What must she keep? This is the common cry of a busy wife and mother's heart, is it not?

Lindsey filled up her thirsty soul in our week together as she sat on the back porch in view of the mountains, poring over Scriptures and writing notes to her heart's content. I saw this friend of mine as content and happy as I'd ever seen her. And she was so incredibly kind to me during this time. Lindsey is a gentle spirit and literally cried tears over my own heartaches suffered in a pain-filled year, holding my hand, praying for me. And when I needed to make a difficult decision, she spoke words so profound that I looked at her luminous dark eyes, paused, then asked, "Lindsey, when did you become wise?"

She laughed, and together we wondered about how indeed we were both growing up into real live women from the girls we once were. We concluded that wisdom is knowledge that has suffered a bit and been softened as a result.

Little did I know that shortly after our time together, Lindsey would deliver a beautiful daughter, Caroline, then slip into a medical nightmare, beginning with a ruptured uterus and uncontrolled bleeding and followed by one life-threatening complication after another. Lindsey spent two months in ICU in a drug-induced coma; she went in to have a baby but ended up in the hospital for three-and-a-half months. Mama went south. At least her body did. But miraculously and against all odds, she survived and is now on the long road to recovery.

But Lindsey's family did not go south. In fact, I told her husband, Tim, that he is the hero Lindsey always proclaimed him to be. And her two oldest daughters, Jacquelyn and Claire, took over the duties of running a home and tending to their younger siblings, Collin and Allison. Jacquelyn chose to return home from her first month of college to become the temporary caregiver for her newborn sister. She and Claire did this as if they were born to be mothers and homemakers, astounding everyone who watched them with their ability and deep commitment and love for their family.

I visited with the children and asked Jacquelyn and Claire how they managed to run the household and take care of their siblings so beautifully. Their reply? "Our mother taught us to do everything with excellence. Besides, family is important."

When Lindsey awoke from her Rip Van Winkle nap to end all naps (and God knows she deserved one), she found that everything she wrote in these pages had been lived out in the flesh by those she'd influenced the most: her family.

Is there a greater tribute?

If Mama Goes South, the title of her book declares, *We're All Going with Her.* In this book she describes how this happens and highlights the importance of a mother's growth and subsequent influence. Yet in light of the irony of this title and Lindsey's own "south," let me offer a new title, though I will agree it's a little wordy: *If Mama Does a Great Job with Her Life and Then Goes South for a Little While, Her Family Will Triumph with the Lessons and Legacy She Gave Them.*

And that, my friends, is why you will want to read and savor these pages.

Not just because they are beautifully written and true. But because the woman who wrote them is a living example of wisdom and joy—lived out in her children, even in the middle of tragedy and crisis.

There is no deeper test for authenticity.

Open this book and get to know and love my friend.

You will be forever changed.

Becky Freeman

1

If Mama Goes South . . .

I think there's a high probability that every woman since Eve has at least *thought* about hurling an object or even running away. Perhaps serene, mild-mannered girls have envisioned just tossing a wooden spoon wickedly into the sink or running into the bathroom, alone, for a full fifteen minutes, while the more demonstrative types have imagined heaving large stones through plate glass and impromptu trips to the Bahamas.

Feeling stressed out with responsibilities and frustrated with the juggling act of being a woman in today's world, or yearning for appreciation from the family or attention and understanding from a work-focused husband is somewhat universal. Is it any wonder that some women are tempted to grab the nearest object and send it sailing?

Take Carol for example. She didn't mean for things to get out of hand, but they did. Literally. Her son ran next door to his grandmother's house and, without knocking, threw open the front door. The conversation went something like this.

"Grandma, come fast!"

Grandma got up quickly from her computer and hurried to her grandson.

"Why, what in the world is wrong?"

"Daddy's got Mama down on the floor."

"What?" The startled grandma's mind raced.

"Grandma, he's pinnin' her down."

Grandma's eyebrows shot up.

"Not a full nelson or anything," he continued. "Well, almost a half nelson. He's sorta holdin' her back, gentle like."

"Holding her back from what?"

"Breakin' dishes."

"Your mother broke a dish?"

"No . . ." His eyes got round as saucers. "She broke half the set!"

Grandma gasped and tried to imagine her intelligent and certainly well-raised daughter and her gentle, mild-mannered son-in-law in such a situation. Surely her grandson was mistaken.

But he wasn't. When she walked in, things were just as Tad had described. Sure enough, a pile of shattered glass was strewn about the floor against one wall, and there sat Jim . . . on Carol. Sort of. He was indeed restraining his wife, gently, as gently as he could while still managing to stop her from hurling dishes through the air.

Carol was not pleased.

Now up until this moment, the entire family and all of their friends would have described both Jim and Carol as nonphysical, lovely people. Carol is extremely articulate, a great verbal jouster who uses words skillfully, never as a lance. Jim is a warm man of few words. Apparently the few words were the problem. He'd done something she disagreed with, and when she began verbally engaging him, he chose to let the matter lie. Like men across time, he remained silent. Failed to engage. Zippo response to her well-worded rebuttal to his actions, which infuriated her even more.

What she wanted was simply to get his attention. As she took dishes out of the dishwasher, she thought how she might accomplish this as her steam began to rise and her dishwasher unloading got louder. Suddenly, plate in hand, it occurred to her what a lovely attention-grabber that dish would make crashing into the wall. But she couldn't. She was a reasonable woman. Highly irate but completely reasonable. Yet, if she threw it just so, aiming for the far wall, nothing else would get broken. So she let it fly. Crash.

She was not prepared for how good that felt. She glanced at Jim, who simply looked at her. Silence. *Not the right response, Jim!* she thought. She sent another plate crashing across the room. And another. Somewhere between the first plate and the end of the set, she got Jim's attention. By the time Carol's mother arrived at the scene, Jim was simply trying to rescue the dinnerware and calm his wife.

Carol's mom felt the situation needed some wise counsel, so she stepped around the entangled couple and across the glass to phone her other daughter, Sharon. She explained the scene.

"Has she lost it, Mom?" Sharon asked.

"I don't know. I don't think so. But how can you tell?"

"Well, what kind of stuff did she throw?"

"Excuse me?"

"Did she throw the good stuff or the Corelle?"

"Uh, the everyday, I think."

"Oh, she's fine then."

15

Now, we don't know exactly how Jim and Carol disentangled themselves from the floor and their dramatic disagreement, but we do know they've returned to their calmer selves, and I daresay Jim listens more and Carol throws less. The moral of this story? We should *never* underestimate the possibilities of a woman headed south, even if her trip is short.

Sometimes in spite of our best efforts we find ourselves heading somewhere we never intended, doing things we never intended, and thinking and feeling things we didn't expect. Sometimes Mama goes south. Not geographically (like Cancun—don't we wish), but figuratively. Sometimes there are seasons when we find ourselves heading south—experiencing a downward, negative turn in our lives where we fall short of living the way we desire or being the person we want to be. Sometimes *life* can go south through tragedy or terrible events beyond our control, and we need people who can help put our broken pieces back together again and serve us in practical ways. During such times we also need the strong arms of our heavenly Father to comfort us and see us through as only he can. But that kind of south is not my focus. I'm discussing when *we* go south; when I go south personally as a woman because of my choices or my complacency.

If someone says, "Have you seen Melba lately? She's really gone south," I doubt Melba would take this as a compliment. A mama who's headed south just might watch Sesame Street for mental stimulation and think the slogan "eat five a day for good health" means five selections from a box of chocolates. But seriously, when a woman is heading south it's not usually a laughing matter.

On the other hand, maybe you enjoy helping yourself to the chocolates only occasionally and you'd never actually throw something in anger or frustration, so you wouldn't consider yourself heading south. In fact, you're not doing too badly. But maybe, deep inside, you long to grow as a woman.

Whether you're heading south, yearning for growth, or lying somewhere between the two, this book can help you tap into your growth potential mentally, physically, and spiritually.

Many Roads South

The road south is a gradual slope. Sometimes we scarcely realize we've lost our visions, laid aside our dreams, or settled into mediocrity in an effort to get by with a little energy intact. But if we're not careful, we may open our bleary eyes to the fact that we're on our way to being far less than we once thought we'd be.

Have you ever needed a change of direction? We all face stresses and distresses, but not one of us ever purposely sets out on a downward journey. We don't get up one day and decide, "Today I think I'll begin to let myself go. I want to look as haggard, unkempt, out-of-date, and wrinkly faced as I can in five years, so I'll start today." We don't wake up and say, "I want to lose it emotionally as often as possible, so how close to the edge can I live?" or "Sanity is so relative. Clear mental processing and intelligent thought just take too much effort." And we never premeditate so distancing ourselves from God that we begin to question his involvement in our lives or even his existence. No. No one intentionally sets out to deteriorate physically, emotionally, mentally, or spiritually. But . . . it happens. The road south is deceptively alluring and surprisingly simple to meander, because it is always the path of least resistance; we usually are on it long before we are even aware we've detoured from the path of ideas and ideals we'd envisioned for our lives.

So how does that happen? How do we begin heading south? Often with a gradual descent along one of the many routes that deteriorate body, soul, or spirit—negative habits, poor attitudes, insane schedules, a continually fruitless spiritual life, lack of tranquility, or sin. We do, say, or think things that tear us down, not realizing that our gradual inclination to berate our husbands, daydream about the "if onlys" in our lives, or compare ourselves with others can sap the life out of us. We go south through the things we choose to hate about ourselves—our body, our accomplishments or lack thereof, and our present circumstances, or even our lot in life in general. We go south through negative things we choose to do and positive things we choose to ignore. Some roads head south because of our lack of knowledge or awareness in a matter. At other times it's because of apathy or bad choices. We have plenty of maps with lots of beautiful routes for life's journey; we just decide it's too difficult to navigate. We lay the map down and opt for an easier route, the path of least resistance. At other times, our trip south is just a side trip, a momentary detour because of unavoidable situations, circumstances out of our control, spiritual attack, or temporary roadblocks we encounter on this life journey.

Some roads south are extremely dangerous. They can lead to a nervous breakdown, nonfunctioning depression, crime and prison, suicidal thoughts, physical or mental illness, even abuse. In the movie *The Ya-Ya Sisterhood,* and in the Italian film *Bread and Tulips,* both main characters are mothers struggling enough to make them run away. They ditch their responsibilities and their families and just leave. And while a part of us may sympathize, deep within we know this is not right. Mothers aren't supposed to leave. These are examples of mothers who have gone south in an over-the-edge way. But many of us struggle, don't we? Some dramatically, others in minor ways—and neither is pleasant.

Other roads south are less grave but still troubling. We find ourselves forty and flabby, wearing far more mileage on our faces than we ever pictured when we were eighteen, spiritually anemic, culturally dead, creatively stifled, bone weary, and painfully undernourished in our souls. These are some possible disappointing destinations when Mama heads south. I know, because I've been there.

It was a time in my life that was as palatable as bran cereal without milk—possible to get through but tough to swallow. I'd felt myself slipping, struggling, groping to cope for a long time. I had three major life projects happening at once—we were building a house and doing much of the work ourselves, I had writing deadlines, and I was attempting to classically educate my four children at home. Any one of those jobs combined with running a household and being a mom is pretty much full time. On top of that, the six of us were living in 1,097 square feet with one dog and two evil cats who took to using the carpet for a litter box. One thousand ninety-seven please-stay-off-my-square-foot, square feet. Oh, I did what I could to juggle timing and prayed about what I was doing that I wasn't supposed to be doing (translation: *God, what can I quit?*), but the bottom line was that God was not releasing me from anything at that point. And to top it all off, I was attempting to do all of that while recovering physically and emotionally from losing a much-wanted baby to miscarriage. The stress was suffocating, the projects demanding, the children needy, and there I was—depleted, depressed. I could feel myself heading south. I didn't even have the energy to hurl a plate.

Here are a few staccato thoughts scribbled in my journal then.

19

I'm depressed.

I'm sad about the baby.

Overwhelmed at the three projects. So what aspect of what project do I do first today?

Worried for Tim, he's working so hard. Angry at the feeling of being a single parent too often in his absence.

I'm physically, emotionally, and spiritually down.

My son is needy, and I have no emotional reserves to do anything. There is no fun, planned or spontaneous. No family time. No reading aloud. Few family dinners. I miss these things. Alli needs to go shopping, and I have no physical energy. I'm dry spiritually.

I want to cry. I can't manage my house very well. Can't keep groceries stocked. In fact, I can't stand the house.

At church, a friend told me she went to bed for a year after her divorce. You can do that? Someone told me this is all impossible. Another friend said my life is very hard compared to hers. Susan said it would put some women in a home. Really? Now that's something I haven't tried yet.

I'm going south and taking the kids with me. Lord, please show me how to change direction.

They're All Going with Her

Why does it matter if we take a little jaunt south? Lots of reasons. Personally we face a loss of contentment, we have less joy, we fall short of the abundant life that Christ has for us, which is a miserable way to live. A woman who's going south also faces lost potential. Who knows what could have been? What she could have become? And most importantly, a woman headed south has lost some of her impact for God's kingdom. But that's not all. Like goslings following a goose, our children take our lead.

One fall day long ago, I walked through the beautiful Public Garden in Boston, enjoying watching the swan boats on the pond and the ducks eating the peanuts the passengers were throwing—a scene that's been happening in Boston for over 120 years. The air was crisp and the leaves were coming into their glorious colors, while back in my Southern hometown things were as hot and green as ever without a hint of a cool breeze.

Then I spotted the famous duck family sculpture, and the day became perfect. Little bronze ducklings followed the mother duck in a line, straight from the pages of my favorite children's classic—Robert McClosky's *Make Way for Ducklings*. I was standing in the book's setting, and it moved me as I looked at the sculpture and thought of my own brood. McClosky had captured a literal and figurative truth that resonates with me as a mother: ducklings follow Mama—across busy streets, into lovely gardens, even south.

I've always been fascinated with the phenomenon called imprinting. Newly hatched ducklings and goslings form an indelible attachment to their mothers—or whatever moving object they encounter if Mother is absent—within days after birth. Imprinting is so powerful that the little birds will follow the mother or mother substitute even through adverse circumstances. If they imprinted on a mother substitute (including humans and wooden decoys) they will continue to follow it in preference to a live duck or goose introduced later. In the movie *Fly Away Home* (loosely based on real research) a little girl adopts a brood of orphaned goslings. She's there when they hatch, so they imprint on her and follow her everywhere. Later when their instincts kick in, telling them it's time to fly south, they have no mother goose to lead the way. So the little girl flies an ultralight plane, and amazingly they follow her . . . south.

Now, if we were to head to sunny south Florida, southern California, the South of France, south of the border, or even south of the house on some days, chances are somebody's going to want to go with us—most likely each and every one of our progeny. These are, after all, the same dear children who for the first few years of their lives thought we needed travel companions to the bathroom. If Mama goes south, they're all going with us! But when the south we're facing is a state of being instead of a warm destination, we'd better take notice.

One night during my "south season," after a week of high anxiety and stress, my kids fell apart. One, in a tearful outburst, ripped up his schoolwork, another suddenly developed a sore throat, a third one came down with a debilitating migraine, and a fourth developed a serious case of bad attitude. All at the same time. What I was dealing with didn't exactly *cause* the sore throat or migraine; perhaps there were logical connections like poor eating and sleeping patterns and spillover stress. Yet it never ceases to amaze me. When I come unglued, they seem to also.

Brenda Nixon, the author of *Parenting Power in the Early Years,* told me one reason why.

There is nothing, *nothing,* moms go through that does not in some way affect their children. Job loss, illness, separation, remarriage, depression, and spiritual struggle—young ones living in the home perceive everything. Children often don't understand what's going on, but they know Mom is different or preoccupied. When Mama "goes south" her parenting skills (patience, humor, perspective) are compromised, which then affects her responses to her children. A vicious cycle is often set in motion of the children misbehaving in an attempt to reconnect with her, and then Mom overreacting.

Our mental and emotional states have been proven to affect our children, especially when we have severe, lingering depression.

When Douglas Teri and his colleagues conducted a study of fifty mother and baby pairs and fifty-four mother and preschooler pairs, they found high rates of insecure attachment among the children of depressed mothers. Eighty percent of the babies and 87 percent of the preschoolers were insecurely attached when their mothers suffered from depression.[1]

The God-given bond between a mother and child, particularly formed early in their life together, is so important that it affects the child's other intimate attachments and their self-identify. In *The Power of Mother Love,* Brenda Hunter says, "Our children will someday leave our presence with core messages about their worth, whether positive or not. And these messages will influence every important decision they make, as well as their capacity to nurture their children."[2]

Our choices have consequences, and our choices as mothers are magnified, because we were designed with the power to shape a life. I call that the trickle-down effect. We influence children physically, mentally, spiritually, and emotionally. If we stuff our cabinets with junk food and set poor examples for healthy eating, we shouldn't wonder when they develop a weight problem. If we use atrocious grammar or are seldom seen cracking a book or discussing a thoughtful idea, we can expect them to follow suit. They also learn matters of the heart and the power of a life on fire for God (or not) from us.

It's true that some kids outshine their upbringing and their education and surpass their parents or succeed against environmental odds stacked against them, but they are most often the exception, and they usually do so with strong motivation and encouragement from someone in their life. But because this sometimes happens does not negate the power of our influence.

Another viewpoint to the trickle-down principle is the argument that says, "Wait a minute. Don't hang the entire responsibility of my child's life on me. He's an adult now telling his therapist he's screwed up because of me." Sometimes parents suffer when their grown children find it easier to *blame* them than to forgive if needed, or to take personal responsibility for their own choices in life. Our influence eventually does give way to their personal choices. Once when my mother was troubled by my brother's actions after he'd left home, she hung a yellow sticky note on her mirror that said, "My children are now responsible for their own choices." She needed to remind herself that she'd done her job. Yet forty-one years after my mother had me, the *thought* of her still influences me.

Brenda Hunter describes this process as internalization—"our children internalize the image of mother that we give them." I love how the writer Jean Hendricks puts it:

> My children tell me that at those times when I was no more than a photograph on the dresser two thousand miles away, I talked in their consciences. I showed up in their habits and decisions. I was there in a front row seat. What an assignment!
>
> In everything from the high chair routine to the bridal parties, I had been teaching something . . . and I had the inside track. Because I was "Mom," I was different; I walked in their hearts whether I wanted to or not. It was critically important that I went in the right direction.[3]

Because walking in our children's hearts is such a privilege, we need to do everything possible to ensure the direction won't be south. I have a tiny figurine of a goose with her goslings lined up behind her; it reminds me to make way for my ducklings, to be careful where and how I walk . . . for my children are following. It's also become a visual of our influence as women; we were designed to impact those we interact with, whether we're mothers or not. As my friend and author Lael Arrington teaches, we can move beyond the *small* story of our personal lives and make an impact in God's *kingdom* story.

So where are you on this grand journey? Are you struggling with stress? Are you content with who you are as a person and with what you do each day? Are there some areas of your life where you see yourself slipping or where you've settled for mediocrity? Are you accomplishing the things you used to dream about? Do you ever spiritually feel like a gourd in the desert . . . dry, dry, dry? Do you wonder if what you do makes a difference, if *you* make a difference? If you feel like "Mama's going south," take heart. God doesn't want us to live this way. He has such a better plan for our lives, one to give us a future and a hope.

An Escape from Going South

During my "southern period" I struggled with much of the above. Stress had a stranglehold on me. I desperately tried to be content, but I had such pockets of longing; I wasn't accomplishing what I wanted to, even though I was doing too much, and my spiritual life was choking on desert sands. I could relate to the woman in *I Don't Know How She Does It* who discovered the fine art of hitting store-bought tarts just so with a rolling pin so they looked homemade, except I was doing good if I even remembered to *buy* the tarts.

Thankfully, God is merciful, and he didn't keep me in that place. Like the gentle Father he is, he gradually led me to a sweeter place, and with hindsight I can now say I learned a great deal. Don't you hate how so often our greatest growth comes through adversity? God gradually answered the cry of my heart I'd penned in my journal, but it was a process; I wanted a quick fix, but God chose to do some character chiseling. One of God's good gifts to us is logic and common sense, so I applied some to find immediate relief—I evaluated my situation, eliminated what I could, delegated what I couldn't, got help where possible, and did only what I was really able to do. It wasn't easy, but I eventually got through that time.

But during it and afterwards, I kept dwelling on some of those questions that make us really evaluate our lives, peeking deep into our souls. I didn't simply want to solve my problems and live a happy life, I wanted to know who I really was and believe I was doing what I was supposed to be doing. I wanted to live in the fullness of the life God had for me, somehow making a difference in my corner of the world. I wanted to grow as a woman. How about you?

Children are delighted with the idea of physical growth. Birthdays are celebrations that mark growth, literally, from my nephew's point of view. On Artyom's sixth birthday he went to the wall that held his growth marks, and his mother measured him. When he turned around and saw the new mark, he suddenly burst into tears. Seems the line had barely moved, and he'd expected to wake up on his birthday and find a big jump on the chart to accompany his new age. He'd anticipated visible physical growth. Of course, we know better as adults—we grow up and discover our desire for visible growth shifts from the physical to the delight of mental, spiritual, and personal growth, which is really the antithesis of going south.

A woman who is growing and learning in body, soul, and spirit is not going south. Oh, we may feel like hurling a plate or running away once in a while, and we will no doubt go through times of difficult life circumstances that detour us from where we want to be. But they can be just that . . . detours, not destinations.

I love these definitions of growth: to spring up and develop to maturity; to be able to grow in some place or situation; to become larger (ignore that part!) and often more complex; to progressively develop; and to obtain influence. A woman who is growing is not just a woman avoiding going south. She's a woman who is developing maturity, growing in whatever situation she finds herself, gaining complexity, progressing in her life, and increasing her ability to influence. Influence for kingdom purposes.

What a beautiful contrast to a woman who's gone south, because that woman has often stopped growing. And if she stops growing, perhaps she might be beginning to die. In the film *The Sixth Sense,* a little boy says, "I see dead people. They don't even know they're dead." Like the little boy, some of us encounter people who haven't seen growth in their lives in so long they don't even know they've begun to die, at least on some level.

Plants grow. Babies grow. And to do so, both need the right nutrients, tender care, the proper environment, and plenty of time in the sun. So do we, in order to grow as women. We need to provide our body, spirit, and soul with things that nourish us, with tender care, with an enriching environment, and we need to soak up life-giving time in the Son. That's what this book is about.

Walk into a Barnes and Noble, grab a latte, and check out the self-help section. You'll find lots of books about self-improvement, self-fulfillment, self-actualization. They talk about growth, but they center on self. Personal growth certainly involves our "self" as we develop, mature, and continue to become, but unlike that country song line, it's not "all about me." There's a reason to grow besides just for our personal benefit—it's the idea of growing to *give*, of living for something, someone, besides ourselves and for someday besides the here and now. Romans 8 in *The Message* puts a "self-focus" in perspective:

> Focusing on the self is the opposite of focusing on God. Anyone completely absorbed in self ignores God, ends up thinking more about self than God. That person ignores who God is and what he is doing. And God isn't pleased at being ignored.
>
> But if God himself has taken up residence in your life, you can hardly be thinking more of yourself than of him. Anyone, of course, who has not welcomed this invisible but clearly present God, the Spirit of Christ, won't know what we're talking about. But for you who welcome him, in whom he dwells—even though you still experience all the limitations of sin—you yourself experience life on God's terms. . . . God's Spirit beckons. There are things to do and places to go!

Growing as a woman is about being all you can be, being more than you are now; it's about becoming. Becoming what God intended, becoming more than you think possible. It's about wondering who you might become in five years, then letting that vision propel your tomorrow and even your today. It's about avoiding apathy and negative habits that take you south and replacing plodding, hurrying, and surviving with purposeful living, fine-tuning, and a recapturing of dreams. When we grow we are saying "I want to be a better person than I am today; I want to know more than I do now, to improve, learn, discover, taste, experience, enjoy, and give." Even if you're in a good place in your life without any traces of going south, can you say, "I don't want to stay the same"? Women who grow, can.

Nobody wants to go south. Our little "ducklings" are too important, our influence in the world is worth too much. In the following three sections we'll look at growth in spirit, body, and soul.

Maybe you long to keep from going south, to grow, but you're not sure how to do that from where you are now. How do we even begin to grow when we're running on empty? Growth from a place of emptiness needs to first be tackled in the realm of our spirits, as we'll see next.

Part 1

Grab the Map and Go

The Spirit

2

How Can I Give When I Have Nothing Left?

Growth from Emptiness

One day while getting in some "girlfriend time" over lunch, my friend looked at me over her glass of Pepsi and said, "There are so many needs to meet as a woman, aren't there?" I sighed in agreement. "There's each individual child, my husband, my home . . . my list is endless, and sometimes while trying to figure out which need to meet first, I just want to go lay in a hammock and read a book."

My friend is not selfish, neglectful, or lazy—far from it. She was just honestly sharing how sometimes being a nurturing, need-meeting, life-giving woman can be tiring. Our many roles can wear us out to the point of emptiness.

Everyone experiences fatigue, most get worn out to some degree, and some of us, sadly, get to the place of depletion where all known and felt reserves are a memory. We stare glassy-eyed at the cavern of emptiness within, wondering how we will manage to . . . and we can't even finish the thought. Manage, period. Yet we know that people still need us. Tasks are uncompleted. Requirements are still required, and work is always waiting. Have you ever faced your day longing for more energy, time, stamina, strength, patience, or resources to accomplish what lies before you? Have you ever fingered through palpable emptiness physically, emotionally, mentally, or spiritually, and wondered, "How can I give when I have nothing left?" Have you ever felt like your reserves were adequate for growing nothing but fungus, and even that was iffy?

The discouraging, limiting black hole of depletion, whether it's in body, soul, mind, or spirit, whether temporary or long term, leaves us looking for a way up and out. Giving may feel impossible, and growth . . . well, does it even cross your mind then? But growth from emptiness is possible, and I want to share a pivotal perspective that I call the Receiver Principle.

I asked a lot of women if they've experienced this giving-from-nothing quandary. I asked stay-at-home moms, professional women, the disorganized and highly organized, feelers and thinkers, and with rare exception the resounding answer was a collective "Duh!"

If you are among the rare exception who *never* faces more in your day than you think you have available, then I'm exceedingly happy for you and I know that you've probably stopped reading by now. For the rest of us, let's get real about the dilemma of being all we are called to be, doing all we are supposed to do, and walking our path with excellence when, frankly, we feel like roadkill.

I would love to see a statistical chart depicting how most women rank regarding their requirements versus their resources. Tasks, service, availability, expectations, and longings on the right side of the chart. Physical, emotional, mental, and spiritual resources on the left. Perhaps a chart like this would show a picture as varied as our circumstances, temperaments, and faith, with the points on life's line graph highlighting our variable conditions. Thriving. Balanced and fulfilled. Slightly off-balance. Balanced but not fulfilled. Stress-free. Minor stressed. Medium stressed. Major stressed. Coping. Overwhelmed. Dwelling in tragedy. Barely surviving.

In the carnival of life we have days, hopefully lots and lots of them, when we amble up to the carnival barker's game booth as he shouts, "Test your strength, little lady. Step right up and let's see what you're made of." We pick up the mallet for a swing. Confidently, we let 'er rip, pounding the hammer down and shooting the metal marker high into the sky, straight to the top, ringing the bell loudly right up there at Balanced and Fulfilled. We smile. The crowd cheers. Then there are those other days, moments, seasons, when we limp forward to heed his call, struggle to lift the mallet, and anemically send the marker to Barely Surviving. We summon our strength and try again. This time it barely moves, registering for all the world to see that we are at Roadkill. We let the mallet slip from our hands. The crowd winces. Some nod in understanding. These are the days when, to use Brennan Manning's phrase, our cheese has fallen off our cracker.

The "Hows" of Emptiness

The scenarios that bring us to ponder how we can give when we have nothing left are myriad. There's the general "Mom" category with variations on this theme: We run three errands then head for piano lessons, mentally going through our grocery list for the quick trip to follow, knowing it will cost twice what we wish and hoping we don't forget the aspirin. The children's voices float past our muddled thoughts.

"She's touching me."

"He won't give me my glasses."

"I'm hungry. Can you die from hunger, Mommy? There's a McDonald's!"

"You missed the turn! You're supposed to drop me off at Luke's house!"

Then the older child choruses in. "Mom, I have play practice at eight, and I need to take cookies. I think eight dozen would feed the cast and crew, don't you? Oh, and please add deodorant to your list. A new toothbrush too. I think the dog chewed mine. And don't forget about my sleepover Friday night. You told me I could. Oh, I forgot to tell you that Dad called and said you absolutely, positively have to get his dry cleaning and deposit that check today, and to remind you that those people are coming over for dinner, okay, Mom? . . . Mom?"

You sigh deeply, try to process all those requests, drive a little faster, and calculate the hours until bedtime.

Then there's the "more to do than I can possibly get done" category. We have multiple projects with high stakes requiring top-notch work and exquisite timing. We know we made these choices and agreed to do all of these things, just not all at once, and we wonder how we got into this predicament. We want to keep our word, not let anyone down, manage well, or certainly better, if only we weren't so exhausted.

Another category is the waves of life crashing one upon the other before we can adequately catch our breath. A teenager makes a series of very bad choices. A relationship wavers. Financial pressures build. Our husband looks for work and tells us to look at the real-estate section for a smaller house. Meanwhile, someone we love goes to the hospital, and we begin a long vigil, spreading our time, energy, and fragile emotions among the crescendo of life's waves.

Then there's the most painful category of all . . . tragedy. Here are some of the things happening right now in the lives of people I care about. One woman has just found out about her husband's long-standing, unthinkable affair, spiraling a long marriage toward divorce. Another friend just returned from her grown daughter's funeral. Her daughter left four children five and under. A mom in my neighborhood grieves over her four-year-old's death. Another friend went to pick out a headstone for her baby not long ago. Stillborn. Just three weeks before her due date. I don't need to read the newspaper to see tragedy.

Our faith can flourish in times of great duress, and hopefully as we mature, we will be able to count it all joy when we endure tribulation. But there are also times when we endure lesser conflicts that seem to suck the life right out of us, and we find ourselves at that unintentional, undesirable point of giving from nothing. Before I offer a new take on this old problem and hold out some hope that God has graciously given me, let's look briefly at some of the reasons we get into this depleted place.

The "Whys" of Emptiness

There are lots of ways *how* to get into the giving-from-nothing dilemma, but *why* do we end up there? Do you recognize any of these causes?

Overcommitment. We take on more than we should. We say yes when we should have said a number of nos, causing our ability to crash into our availability. Our emptiness is a consequence of our choices.

Lack of balance. We intently focus on one area of our lives, neglecting others. Priorities in our hearts conflict with those reflected in our hours.

Motivation. We want to be a Mary and sit at Jesus' feet, but down deep, we still empathize with Martha. We wonder what's wrong with asking for a little help when there's so much to do. Or maybe, when we're brave enough to let introspection take us to the place of real honesty, we admit to ourselves that we are depleted because all our doing arises out of our love of the sound of the cheering carnival crowd watching us hit the bell.

Sin. We get locked into a lifestyle fueled by sin that we either don't recognize or are unwilling to give up, and we wonder why the vitality of our life ebbs. We blame our temperament: "It's how God made me." We justify our actions: "If only you knew." We use culturally acceptable phraseology for what Jesus calls sin.

Job's plight (and this "ain't heaven"). Sometimes depletion is the result of testing, trying, refining, and pruning at God's hand or with his permission; it is unrelated to our sin or choices. Sometimes we struggle with emptiness and depletion because under God's sovereignty things in this fallen world happen to us.

Ignored basics. We fail to recognize and act upon the simple premise that there is an undeniable link between the mind, body, and spirit, and we ignore basics that are vital to keeping us filled and functioning. That is what this book emphasizes. Sometimes we need to shut up, back off, and get back to basics, as my friend Brenda Koinis suggests. "I believe strongly in

38

the mind/body/spirit connection. I know that I'm not the only woman in the world who feels like crying sometimes when I'm really, really tired. Lately, I've been hearing from God, 'Shut up and back off.'"

Here's what she means.

1. *Shut up.* When we're depleted we often just need to keep our mouths shut and avoid mistakes. Instead of embarking on major discussions or engaging in confrontation, we can choose to be quiet, saving issues for when our reserves are built back up. In this way we can avoid unnecessary conflict and sometimes even find that the issues go away.
2. *Back off.* At other times our emptiness is because we've overstepped our boundaries in others' lives. We've given too much. We may have done more than our share of chores, spent too much emotionally over someone else, or done more than necessary. We must watch for the difference between meeting our family's needs and overmothering.
3. *Check the basics.* We need to maintain the balance of basics. Food. Rest. Sweat. Sex. Sun. Spiritual development. Often adjusting our barometer of these things fills us back up.

The body and soul issues are parts 2 and 3 of this book, so let's return to issues of the spirit—specifically, a potential faith-dissolving conflict we often face when we're headed south.

A Dangerous Conflict

When we find ourselves asking "How do I give when I have nothing left?" we would be wise to go through a mental checklist. How'd I get here? (General "mom stuff," choices, life's waves, tragedy?) Why? (Was it my overcommitment, imbalance, motivations, sin, being human in a fallen world, or ignoring the basics?) By all means, we should do all we can to recognize the cause of the emptiness. We must repent of sin if we want to bear fruit. And learning to make wise choices brings maturity and peace. But, dear friend, please, please don't stop at the mental checklist. We can make ourselves crazy trying to analyze the hows and whys of our depletion.

The thought *I have nothing to give* hurls like a full-body slam into the thought *But I'm commanded by God to give, aren't I?* Unresolved, the emptiness/command-to-give conflict can lead to a crisis of faith. We may sincerely believe and perhaps have even experienced the spiritual truths that God's grace is sufficient, that "greater is he that is in me," that his strength is perfected in our weaknesses. And yet on an "I have nothing to give" day, we may just struggle with applying what we believe to our situation.

If God's commands and promises seem to be in conflict, we risk becoming disillusioned, angry, confused, and depressed. Camping out in this conflicted place can lead to two responses. In one, we look for the answer to our conflicts in ourselves and "works." "With God as my witness, I'll never be depleted again. Now what can I *do?*" Or we can become bitter with God. "I'd really like to go north, God, but my resources have gone with the wind, so as soon as I can get my feet on terra firma or you change my circumstances, we can talk."

When we struggle, we must go back to our beliefs in the matter, for beliefs determine behavior. We must return to truth, and "I have nothing to give" is not truth. We may *feel* that way, but it's not true in actuality. What is true is best explained in the pivotal perspective I mentioned earlier.

The Receiver Principle

Let me hold out to you a sliver of insight that God gave me, a bit of truth that is crucial for any woman who has gone south and feels she has nothing left to give: We are first of all receivers, not givers. We must change our thinking from "I'm a giver" to "I'm a receiver." The Scripture says, "And God is able to make all grace abound to you, so that always having all sufficiency in everything, you may have an abundance for every good deed" (2 Cor. 9:8). God is sufficient! And he can give us abundance! In fact, he already has: "I have received everything in full and have an abundance; I am amply supplied" (Phil. 4:18). And John 1:16 says, "From the fullness of his grace we have all received one blessing after another" (NIV).

I used to get hung up on a verse that I thought indicated the opposite of this truth, that we shouldn't expect to receive things from God. James 1:7 says, "For that man ought not to expect that he will receive anything from the Lord." I was taking this verse out of context (a dangerous practice) and reading it as "don't *expect* to receive." Back up though and read verses 5–8, which describe asking God for wisdom. "[Ask] in faith without any doubting, for the one who doubts is like the surf of the sea, driven and tossed by the wind." The very next verse is the one I stumbled on. When the verse is placed in context, the emphasis changes. "For that man ought not to expect that he will receive . . ." *That* man—the one who doubts and is double-minded and unstable—should not expect to receive, and is contrasted with the one who asks in faith.

It is by faith that we receive and know that we are not empty! Even when we feel as empty as a hole in the ground, we must kick out the doubts, climb up on the bedrock of

41

what we know to be truth, and exercise our faith. We are receivers!

That perspective change, from "I am a giver (no wonder I'm weary)" to "I am a receiver," was a paradigm shift for me. In the echoing cavern of emptiness, I had been focusing on the vastness of the nothingness and wondering how I was ever going to be able to give from *that* place. Instead I've learned, and continue to learn, to focus on all the ways that I am a receiver. Then I realize I am not empty at all! The emptiness is an illusion of feeling and circumstances. In fact, everything we have is from God! "Every good thing given and every perfect gift is from above, coming down from the Father of lights" (James 1:17). Of myself, I have nothing to give. My ability to give comes from what I've been given.

But wait, you may think. *People who do not have a relationship with Christ certainly give.* Yes, but all they have to give is still from God, they just don't recognize it. Their energy, talents, and very life are from God, whether they choose to acknowledge that truth or not.

Recognizing that we are receivers goes beyond determining to count our blessings when we feel empty. Though it is easy to recognize present blessings, awareness of being a receiver should be for blessings present and future. We need not only to count our blessings but also to trust that there will be more. Not only sufficient blessings, but abundant, overflowing, can't-keep-track-of-them-all blessings. That is expanded thinking. We can then stare down the emptiness and shout, "I am a receiver because of what I've already been given! And because I am a receiver now, I will continue to receive from God in the future."

And as our faith-induced proclamation echoes off the walls of our cave while we stand enveloped in the sensation of our emptiness, we will find that simply stepping up on the bedrock of what we truly believe has shifted our focus from feelings to truth. "I am a receiver who gives from the overflow of what God gives me!" Bask for a moment in this place, this solid ground of belief from which behavior flows.

There are two ways in which we can fail to receive, however. The first is when we feel so needy, so empty, that all we do is focus on the lack, seeing only the emptiness rather than our Source who supplies our needs. We see only physical reasons for our depletion and ignore the deeper spiritual aspect of the problem. It may be true that at times our lack *is* simple and physical (like feeling depleted because we need more sleep), but there is a danger in being too self-sufficient, in examining how and why we feel empty and only looking pragmatically for the way out, instead of finding God's truths that will reveal how full we really are, how sufficient and faithful God really is to us.

The second is when we fail to realize the depth of our need. As my friend Craig Smith, a pastor and speaker, says, "We don't realize how desperately we need what God has to give." In the classic devotional called *Waiting on God*, Andrew Murray makes a similar point and talks about receiving from God:

> Because believers do not know their relationship to God of absolute poverty and helplessness, they have no sense of the need of absolute and unceasing dependence, or the unspeakable blessedness of continual waiting on God. But once a believer begins to see it, and consent to it, he by the Holy Spirit begins each moment to receive what God each moment works. . . . God unceasingly gives and works as His child unceasingly waits and receives. This is the blessed life.[1]

Two disciplines lead to the benefits of the Receiver Principle, of living the "blessed life": counting your blessings

and focusing on the character of God. One stirs up grati-
tude, the other stirs up hope; together they stir up faith.

Count Your Blessings

Have you ever made an actual list of your blessings?
I mean really listed as many good things as you could
think of? I highly recommend this astounding exercise! If
we count ourselves Christian women who have accepted
the gift of eternal life that Jesus' death and resurrection
paid for, acknowledging our sin and need for a Savior and
desire to follow him, then the first thing we can mark on
our list of things received is eternal life. But what else
have we received?

- Jesus and God the Father (Matt. 10:40; 18:5)
- An abundance of grace (Rom. 5:17)
- Rewards (Matt. 10:41; 1 Cor. 3:8)
- Miracles (Matt. 11:5)
- The Holy Spirit (John 20:22; 1 Cor. 2:12)
- The Word (1 Thess. 1:6)
- The crown of life (James 1:12)
- Peace (John 14:27)
- Victory over our flesh (Gal. 5:24)
- Comfort (John 14:16)
- Help (Ps. 118:7)
- Joy (John 15:11)
- Power (Eph. 3:20)
- Good gifts (Matt. 7:11)
- Attention from God (1 Peter 3:12)
- God's nearness (James 4:8; Ps. 119:151)
- Friendship (John 15:15)

- Forgiveness (Acts 26:18)
- Life (John 5:24)
- An inexplicable, everlasting love from the Lover of our souls, God himself (Jer. 31:3)
- Promises upon promises! (2 Cor. 1:20)

Even that, friends, is an incomplete list. God's gifts to us, all that we have received and are able to receive from him, are like a beautiful, refreshing river. In my attempt to describe it, I have just reached into the river with my small tin camping cup, filled it, and offered you a sip. What's in the cup is but a small taste of the sweetness and vastness of the river. And so it is with God's gifts, the bounty we receive and already have received from him.

Any one of those gifts, already given to us as believers in Christ, can be life changing, even in a place of emptiness. Especially in that place. We have been given grace and forgiveness and peace. We have received and do receive love, even when we don't have it all together. No need to clean up first. No matter our condition, God loves us. To be the recipient of someone's love is sweet and wonderful and empowering. To have that love from the Creator of the universe is life changing. Counting our blessings is powerful. Now for the next discipline in understanding the Receiver Principle.

Focus on the Character of God

The spirit is every bit as real as the body and soul. Embracing the spiritual view may do more for you than any practical action step, any how-do-I-fix-my-situation activity. Why? It takes us back to the character of God. To truth. To the reality of these things he tells us:

Peace I leave with you.

You are more than conquerors.

I will be your comforter.

Greater is he that is in you than he that is in the world.

My grace is sufficient for you, for my power is perfected in weakness.

On days when we feel empty, we need to remember to focus on God's character and the reality of all he has given, has to give, and delights to give us. We can fix our minds on his great love, his infiniteness, his lovingkindness, and his desire for our good. God is the source of everything good, and all that we need we can receive from him. John Calvin wrote about this in *The Institutes of the Christian Religion:*

> Moreover, although our mind cannot apprehend God without rendering some honor to him, it will not suffice simply to hold that there is One whom all ought to honor and adore, unless we are also persuaded that he is the fountain of every good, and that we must seek nothing elsewhere than in him. This I take to mean that not only does he sustain this universe (as he once founded it) by his boundless might, regulate it by his wisdom, preserve it by his goodness, and especially rule mankind by his righteousness and judgement, bear with it in his mercy, watch over it by his protection; but also that no drop will be found either of wisdom and light, or of righteousness or power or rectitude, or of genuine truth, which does not flow from him, and of which he is not the cause. *Thus we may learn to await and seek all these things from him, and thankfully to ascribe them, once received, to him* [emphasis mine]. . . . For until men recognize that they owe everything to God, that they are nourished by his fatherly care, that he is the Author of their every good, that they should seek nothing

beyond him, they will never yield him willing service. Nay, unless they establish their complete happiness in him, they will never give themselves truly and sincerely to him.

When we focus on the character of God—the great giver of all things—we have every reason to hope that God not only will but *delights* to continue to give to us so that we may give to others. When that hope leads us to faith, we will feel our cup overflowing.

Growth from Emptiness

Growth is an increased capacity to receive. The more we grow the more we are able to receive, just as our children eat more as they grow. And when we are growing, we are receiving things like

- new beliefs
- increased faith
- greater understanding
- knowledge
- insight
- intimacy
- skill or ability
- wisdom
- love
- restoration
- fruit of the Spirit

This receiving creates abundance in our lives. From this abundance we have more than we need and are able to give from God's overflowing goodness to us.

47

Here's the equation: Receiving = growth = abundance = overflow = giving. As I said earlier, I am a receiver who gives from the overflow of what God gives me! Remembering this receiver principle and maintaining a balance in the body/spirit basics discussed earlier is how we can give when we feel like we have nothing left and can attain growth from emptiness.

Stressing the spiritual needs in dealing with depletion is the first line of defense, yet it is true that in this life there may be times when God is calling us to sojourn in a hard place for a season. We may simply be in a time when we need practical help—someone else to lift us up, help bear our burden for a bit. If *everyone* were always a burden bearer, there would be no one with burdens for us to bear. Admitting our need and accepting such help is as biblical as being the one who gives. When a mom has a critically ill husband or child in the hospital for an extended period of time and other children at home to care for, she may well encounter those "nothing to give" moments. She doesn't need to be told to check the reasons she feels this way. She needs a meal, a nap, and help from Jesus' servants . . . us.

But when we are simply dealing with the pressures of modern life and its frantic pace, we can replace our potential for frustration or bitterness with God by reflecting daily on truth, his character, and the myriad ways that we are receivers. There we'll find the realness of his grace, the sufficiency of his strength, the comfort of his love. From this place comes growth!

But what do we do when we understand these things in our heads, but our spiritual lives still seem wanting? Sometimes, in spite of our knowledge and understanding, we have times when we feel spiritually dry. We'll look at ways to quench that dryness next.

3

What Am I Doing in the Desert?
Quenching a Dry Spirit

I know the desert has its own unique beauty, that some people were born for the heat. I'm just not one of them. It's the cool mountains that nourish my soul. Four seasons delight me, even snow. I'll take green over rocks any day. Pastures over sand. Hills over flatness. I don't want a desert. I want a garden.

And so it is in my spirit life. I want it healthy and growing. Yet why have I looked around on more than one occasion these past forty years and wondered, *What am I doing in the desert? How did my spirit get so . . . dry?*

Have you ever been in a spiritual desert? Have you ever experienced dry words in the Scriptures and prayers that seemed to stall near the ceiling? The activities, service, ministry, and work that used to give you such a sense of purpose and joy has waned and now brings neither. Maybe you've gone through the motions—church attendance, singing, teaching a class. Why, you've even worked in the nursery. But it was just that—motions. You're not sure when the heart went out of it.

For many people, the sense of void in the spirit side of their person drives them to God. We are created to realize that there's more to this life than what our eyes can see, bodies can feel, and day-timers can manage. Deep within us lies a longing to understand who we are and our place in this world and to know that there's something, someone bigger than we are. This longing propels us to search for God. A search that ends with a promise as we see in Jeremiah 29:13: "You will seek Me and find Me when you search for Me with all your heart." When we find him, we discern the richness and life of our spirits deeply connected to God's Spirit, and experience joy, fruit, and growth in our spiritual lives in Christ. But then slowly or suddenly, briefly or for a season, the joy diminishes and we find dry toast where we used to banquet . . . that is a desert.

"Why don't I feel close to you, God?" we ask. "Why can't I experience you doing anything in my life?" In our spirits we may feel almost nothing. We may watch others experience God while we stand on parched ground, observers with dusty sandals at the edge of others' gardens, and wonder, "What am I doing in the desert?"

In trying to find that answer, I sort through different voices in my head, each one eager to point out how and why I missed Palm Springs and am now in Death Valley. The Church Lady in my mind purses her lips and looks over her glasses. "How'd you ever let yourself get here? You know the desert is no place for a lady. Now find your map that you obviously lost and do whatever it takes to get back to greener pastures." Her younger sister, Thoroughly Modern Millie, who never misses Bible study and always has ready insights to my pain, adjusts her black-and-white outfit and agrees. "There's so much life in the spirit. Just figure out what you're doing wrong and stop. Disobedience led you to the desert." Then they both disappear, glad to be truth-tellers.

Now Grace appears, stirs her sweet tea, and oozes, "But darlin', you didn't know you were in the desert. How could you? The signs were so unclear. Besides, you've hurt no one. You just take your time on this road."

Then that neighbor who drives a Jag and never looks flustered or sweaty glides in front of Grace and softly says, "You know, the desert's not so bad. With life being so busy, what's wrong with just lying by the pool, sipping a fruit thing with those little umbrellas, and not doing or thinking anything? You don't want to exert yourself. Besides, once you're there, it's just so easy to stay and stay."

Next, my friend from the health club who's not sure she believes in God looks wistfully at me and says, "How'd your spirit get dry? You mean it's not supposed to be that way?"

At last their voices fade away, and I hear Uncle Henry, who sips endless cups of coffee at the family reunion and tells great stories without ever breaking stride in his dominoes game. "Hon," he says, "in the end, it doesn't really matter how you got yourself in the desert. It's on the map in a few places if you look carefully. So long as you know there's a garden on the other side of it."

So I wave their voices from my head by thinking hard about the tuna casserole in the oven, but when it's done and I open the oven door, the dry heat rushes into my face and reminds me once again that I really do hate the desert. I let the voices line up like a receiving line while I inspect their comments for kernels of truth. Millie and the Church Lady have a handle on "doing" Christianity and are right about the disobedience, but just at the moment I'm not exactly sure what I did wrong. Even though I found a kernel of truth, I feel like smacking them, ever so lightly.

Grace is right too in that there weren't any signs that I was headed for a spiritual desert, but she's only holding a half kernel, because I know it does matter how long I stay, even though I so appreciate her compassion. The neighbor with the Jag is right about how it feels good sometimes to just stay in the desert, but I know it's not supposed to be my destination. And my friend who's searching for God reminds me that I am too.

But dear Uncle Henry hasn't handed me just a kernel, he's given me a whole delicious earful; my desert might be on God's map, yet there's great hope. The garden's just around the bend. And I begin to remember what it's like to be spiritually refreshed, growing, fruitful. So I plod on, knowing my dry spirit will be quenched.

So How Did We Lose the Map?

So how *did* we lose our way and end up in this desolate place? Perhaps we've been so busy and have simply forgotten to look at our map because so many other things came first and, well, here we are.

Or maybe we've chosen to ignore the map, left it right in that glove box even though we knew the scenery was changing. But we didn't care. We felt justified, and we hold up our anger and our hurt as proof. "But God," we say, "you remember what he did to me?" or "It's not like nothing happened—she died, you know." Our anger and hurt and pain lock the map away, and we find ourselves wandering into drier and drier places. A scary thing about the desert is that sometimes we don't even realize things are becoming a bit parched; we're tooling along in our Range Rover with the AC cranked up, sipping sugary sodas, oblivious to the climate change because we're so very comfortable for the moment, rushing along in our jam-packed life.

But sooner or later, the AC peters out, the sugary substitutes in our lives start to taste saccharin, and the cushy ride chokes and sputters to a stop, forcing us to realize that facing the desert afoot is an entirely different matter. It's hot. We're sweaty. We can hardly breathe. We're parched and desperate for a drink. At about that point we decide it's no fun sucking on a dry canteen. No fun at all. And suddenly we experience thirst, precisely what we needed all along.

Although going south spiritually is a long and winding road, let's look at three areas in which we can get back on the right track spiritually: our disciplines, doing, and devotion. First let's define terms. By "disciplines" I mean *spiritual habits* like prayer (not discipline as punishment in this instance), by "doing" I mean the things we do for God in serving him, and by "devotion" I simply mean our love for him (not the definition implying a short spiritual reading or quiet time).

Disciplines

When we realize our spirits are dry, often the first place we look is to our spiritual disciplines—what used to be called the "religious exercises" of prayer, Bible study, meditation, and fasting. In *Celebration of Discipline*, Richard Foster writes inspiringly about the inward, outward, and corporate disciplines of the Christian life as the path to spiritual growth. The ones I mention above are inward disciplines, and our spirits will feel parched when we neglect them.

Prayer is that two-way communication with the God who made and loves us. A soul who does not pray is a soul living in silence. As in a marriage, that's only okay for a time; then the lack of communication begins to take its toll. Reading and studying God's Word is life, while extended neglect of this discipline brings barrenness. Meditating on its truths, stopping our bodies and thought lives long enough to allow this teaching, instruction, wisdom, reproof, correction, and love letter to us from God to enter our hearts and minds, is a rich discipline indeed. With it we grow, without it we shrivel. And fasting is that often overlooked exercise that many of us relegate to the lives of ancient believers or any denomination other than ours. (More on fasting in a later chapter.)

Author and evangelist David Wilkerson wrote that maintaining a prayer life is key to overcoming dry times (along with not being afraid of a little suffering). He said:

> Nothing dispels dryness and emptiness more quickly than an hour or two shut in with God. Putting off that date with God in His secret closet causes guilt. We know our love for Him should lead us into His presence; but we busy ourselves in so many other things, then time slips away, and God is left out. We throw in His direction a whole array of "thought prayers." But nothing can take the place of that secret closet with the door shut, praying to the Father in that seclusion. That is the solution to every dry spell.[1]

Doing

As women, we know "doing" well, don't we? Do the laundry, do the dishes, do that project right now. How are you doing? What may I do for you? And so it goes until we've checked off all our to-do's . . . until tomorrow. It seems to never end. Usually we're very good at it. Sometimes it makes us crazy. It seems the doing that fills our days and the attitude with which we attack the doing tells a great deal about where we are on the desert/ garden path. Do our activities reflect our priorities? Is our doing self-focused or others focused? Is our time mostly spent on our vocations and avocations, or do we truly make enough time for the people in our lives? And how do we *feel* about all the caregiving we do? "I had to bake eight stupid pies for the church auction, Marge. Eight! Can you believe that? No wonder nobody makes piecrust from scratch anymore . . ." And we rack one up for martyrdom. "When I got home today, I picked up the house, got dinner on (one for us, two for those people at church), went to hospital visitation, and then came home and planned the women's class for the next three months. You know, Marge, Mabel tried to get someone else to do that, but she *knows* that's been my job for ten years . . ." And we relish the sore arm we get from polishing our halos. Clearly, the great challenge of our doing is knowing what to do and when, in the right balance of our gifting, time, availability, calling, and need, and with pure motives for Christ's kingdom purposes.

Francis de Sales, a late-sixteenth-century writer who greatly influenced the Western Church, wrote in his *Introduction to the Devout Life* about charity—the ability to do good derived from love for God. He encouraged that charity be done "carefully, frequently, and promptly," not as if we were ostriches who never fly, or hens who fly infrequently and clumsily near the ground, but as eagles who fly high and often. Some people exercise disciplines and practice spiritual "doing" in actions that outwardly look holy, but he calls these "phantoms of devotion" in reality.

Sometimes we tuck our "doing" away on a shelf, absorbed in self, ignoring the fact that love is a verb, an action word. Perhaps we shouldn't wonder at our desert state if our actions are continually missing, if our ability to do good and serve with love is passive and altogether unverblike.

In contrast, I like how de Sales describes a Christian's ability to do difficult things such as serving others when we're tired or caring for the sick or restraining anger. He writes that our goal is for the world to see us performing rigorous tasks like "the bees amid the banks of thyme. They find there a very bitter juice, but when they suck it out, they change it into honey because they have the ability to do so." I want to be less like the inner voices of Mabel and Marge, complaining or taking pride in the things I do for God, and more like that bee, able to perform the tasks God gives, drawing sweetness from bitterness because he enables me. Or as de Sales put it, sweetening bitterness in our works with the true spiritual sugar of our devotion.

Danger Alert

These disciplines and doing of our inner and outer lives can and should be practiced and even celebrated, as Richard Foster's book title suggests. They will be an inevitable product of our blooming, growing garden. Yet at times if we find ourselves walking outside the Range Rover down a dusty path and looking for the map through the discipline/doing route, let me echo the words of Steve Irwin, that crazy snake-handling, alligator-wrangling Australian: "Danejuh, danejuh, danejuh!"

Danger indeed. One inclination when we sense a desert-on-foot experience coming on is to immediately examine the disciplines of our prayer lives, Bible reading, meditations, and so on. Another inclination when we taste dryness is to pout or pull away from God because we inwardly long for the sweet and savory. Why read the Bible if it's dry, and why pray if we see no answers? Or perhaps we try to overcome a dry spirit by pouring ourselves afresh into our doing. *If I can just* do *enough for God, this desert will pass,* we think, so we expend much energy and time into this part of our outer lives. But from this barren place our doing becomes drudgery, the desert heats up, and burnout awaits upon the hill. Trying to escape the desert by focusing on the disciplines and doing alone will leave us sucking on that dry canteen—parched, unsatisfied, and as much in the desert as we ever were. Instead, our sights should be focused on devotion—our simple love of God and realization of his great love for us.

Devotion

I love the clarity in a well-defined word. Devotion means strong attachment or affection, or the state of being devoted, which means to apply attention, time, or oneself completely. That's my goal in devotion to God. One thing I've observed in reading Christian works written several hundred years ago or more is the frequent *assumption* of this mutual love relationship with God in a believer's life. When Francis de Sales wrote about devotion, he centered his meaning of the word on *charity.* Love for God was assumed. He addressed his words to "Philothea," meaning one who loves God: "Genuine living devotion, Philothea, presupposes love of God, and hence it is simply true love of God."[2] Another writer described de Sales's take on "true devotion" as horizontal, the strength to serve others, and as vertical, the "head-over-heels" white-hot love of God.[3]

I look around at the church of today and wonder about this. Would these writers find such assumptions in our current world, where we have so much and need so little? Can we look at today's church at large and presuppose a deep, passionate love of God in the majority? Does the world see a church culture filled with those who are genuinely in love with Jesus? Can I look into my own heart and see with consistency that white-hot love?

That white-hot love of God is my key to the glove box to unlock the map that leads me out of the desert. *That* is what I mean by devotion. And longing for God is the place to begin. "Therefore the LORD longs to be gracious to you, and therefore He waits on high to have compassion on you. For the LORD is a God of justice; how blessed are all those who long for Him" (Isa. 30:18).

Consider these three things about that road from the desert to the white-hot place: what we really want, why God allows us in the desert, and how to quench the dryness.

What We Really Want

Sometimes it's a distance from God that characterizes our desert experience with him; at other times hurt and pain lead us there. But we don't always know the difference. We don't know just how or when we lost the map, and we find the distance and pain can overlap, their sands mingling in a barren desolation of soul. Our dry spirit longs for two things, the emotional and the supernatural—feelings and experience. We want to *feel* God. We want to *experience* him as if he were walking into our natural world and pulling up a chair beside us. One summer night in Atlanta, both happened to me.

I was in a very public venue when a very private thing happened. I'd come to a crowded convention, excited to see longtime friends and lead a workshop. I also reveled in the new life growing within me. After two years of praying, my husband and I had decided to have another child, which was significant considering my "maturity." I wasn't quite as old as Abraham's Sarah, but I wasn't Ken's Barbie either. I was, in fact, pregnant and euphoric. Then something went wrong. Far away from home and my husband, I was whisked away to Emory hospital in Atlanta.

Sometimes God reaches down and loves us in the physical world through his children, and he did that for me in Atlanta by sending my good friend Lael and her friend Patty to be with me. Lael was my comfort. Patty helped me physically in ways Lael could not, even though she was a complete stranger to me. Let's just say we bonded quickly. I was in trouble, and God knew I needed physical help, emotional strength, and a healthy dose of laughter amid tears. In the emergency room between my tears and far too early contractions, Patty walked in carrying a bouquet of flowers, interesting considering it was Sunday night.

"Oh, thank you!" I said. "How did you—"

"Oh, I got them off that desk over there," Patty answered. "You need them far more than she does." She put the flowers in my lap and wheeled me down the hall after the nurse while I watched for hospital security. When the staff took their sweet time bringing me pain relief, she threatened to sail to the nurses' station in Shirley MacLain mode, a la *Terms of Endearment*, pounding on the counter and yelling, "It's time for her medicine *now!*" Later in an ER room with Lael and a doctor, she appeared, bearing another "hot" vase of ivy with a bow. "Thought you needed these, hon," she said and walked out. "Who's that?" the doctor asked. Patty stuck her head back in the door and remaining straight-faced said, "I'm her florist."

I closed my wet eyes and lowered my head, shoulders shaking. The doctor reached out to console me, but I think he suspected I was laughing through tears when Lael lost her attempt not to laugh and ended up snorting in her Dr. Pepper. God had sent me a personal florist who impersonates Shirley MacClain and a spiritual giant friend to be with me in my crisis. He is so creative! He let me feel his touch emotionally, through laughter and tears, and physically, with the practical help of friends.

Later that night when I felt what I'd prayed for slip from my body, I knew a created life had just ceased to be. Knew it long before the technician's sterile proclamation of "no viable pregnancy." Knew it in that deep-inside-of-you place that surfaces when you find yourself alone. After my friends had to leave, I waited alone for the operating room and general anesthesia.

Through a thin haze of pain and medication, the palpable sense of aloneness, of loss, left me breathless. I closed my eyes and lay still. Then, in he walked. His presence immediately calmed me. He simply sat in the chair next to me, his vigil begun. I wasn't alone anymore. Wasn't afraid. I knew who he was long before I noticed his robe dragging the floor.

It's the morphine, I thought. Of course, skeptics would say. Yet I knew then what I knew clearly the next morning. Whether in my mind's eye, or simply an awareness in my spirit, I'd felt Jesus' presence. God had lifted the curtain to allow me a dim peek at the supernatural walking into my natural world and pulling up a chair.

Sometimes we need help in our physical reality. Sometimes we long for a peek at the supernatural. That night God allowed me both. I'd come to Atlanta so full of life and had left so very empty, except for that moment sandwiched between grief when I experienced God's love.

We want to feel God in our daily lives, we want to experience the supernatural working, but that's not always the case, is it? We go through life with the curtain usually drawn between the supernatural and ourselves. We occasionally find ourselves emotionally flat-lined, devoid of the experience or feeling of God in our lives, at least on the surface. We long for it not to be so, long to feel God, long for the emotions or the experience of a white-hot love for God. I was grateful to experience his presence that night, but I'm also glad that my faith doesn't rest on just my feelings and emotions.

Our postmodern world focuses on the experiential, yet as thinking Christians we must not *depend* on feelings and emotions. It is wonderful to feel God's presence and experience him in our lives, but that is not the crux of our faith. We must be a people of reason who, unlike cultural postmoderns, know and depend on absolute truth. We can know God is there, even if we can't feel him. Such reason can get us through our dry times.

In a column titled "More Doctrine, Not Less," Chuck Colson advocated challenging postmodernism, which has "rejected not only God and reason, but also the very idea of universally valid truth." He took issue with a Christian speaker who'd recommended not fighting with postmodernity but taking advantage of it by declaring experience over reason and image over words.

> Some Christians—like that conference speaker—think we should join the postmodern bandwagon's emphasis on experience. One pastor told me that 10 years ago he could discuss moral truth with unbelievers, while "today I connect only on grounds of pain and compassion." But connecting only at the level of feelings is a weak reed for evangelism. . . . The Gospel is not a matter of soothing feelings or rewarding experiences (although it may produce both). It is the Truth that postmodernists can stake their lives on.[4]

And it is knowing that Truth, unchanging and absolute, that can get us through our desert times when our spiritual feelings and experiences are wanting.

When we find ourselves in a desert, we want out as fast as possible, but before we look at how to quench that dry spirit, let's consider the possibility that sometimes we aren't supposed to escape the desert immediately.

Why God Allows Us in the Desert

When we're in that place, the most natural reaction is to want to get out. It's hot and sweaty and, frankly, anyone would rather be drinking deeply than in this desolate place, sucking on a dry canteen. But before we go nuts trying to figure out how we got here and how to get out, picture two deserts, two roads. On one, we're there simply because we got lost. On the other, we're there because we were led. Sometimes God wants us to sojourn in the desert a while. He's not being mean, he's got a plan, and it's to teach us, grow us, work out our weaknesses, and make us more like him.

Are you familiar with the "dark night of the soul"? This common expression came from the most famous work of John of the Cross, a late-sixteenth-century monk and writer who wrote his work by that name while in prison. His dark night of the soul describes a spiritual desert, a place where one loses all pleasure experienced in devotional life. He describes well the reasons God would lead us to dryness (the main reason being to purify us), and some of our imperfections that lead to our deserts: secret pride when we are quite satisfied with our spiritual selves; an attachment to the feelings we get from our devotional lives; our effort at being a "saint in a day"—busy doing in order to recover lost joy, being a spiritual sloth who abandons spiritual exercises when the pleasure we get out of it is lost; and spiritual envy when we only revel in our own growth.

"The Lord heals such souls through the aridity of the dark night," writes John of the Cross.

> God perceives the imperfections within us, and because of his love for us, urges us to grow up. . . . He weans us from all of the pleasures by giving us dry times and inward darkness. . . . No soul will ever grow deep in the spiritual life unless God works passively in that soul by means of the dark night.[5]

Some deserts are not meant for immediate escape, and yield beautiful fruit in our lives. Before we get busy trying to find the exit map, we need to look around at what God wants to teach us in barrenness. We can endure the desert when we know he has a purpose and when hope for the garden of growth ahead blooms within us.

Quenching a Dry Spirit

A thousand theologians and fifteen mildly thoughtful souls with heartbeats might answer with 1,015 variants on the how-to-quench question. So I offer another. Any truth to it is simply found in what aligns with God's Word, the plumb line of truth.

One day, I was sitting on my bed, thinking deep thoughts, when it occurred to me to grab a pen. I often write prayers, and sometimes I hear an answer. I wrote:

> God, here I am again, in that place that eventually leaves me gasping and scrambling for a way out. You know I hate these dry times, that I yearn for a garden of soul, ripe with

fruit, so I wonder. Why do my feelings seem so detached from my experience with you?

I stopped writing and reflected on a recent worship service, where I'd tried, really tried, to touch some emotion in my worship, knowing that worship is a major key, next to devotion, to unlock the glove box that contains the map. My trying was for naught.

I don't feel close to you now, Lord. How can we reestablish some intimacy here?

Then I stopped and read what I had just written about feelings being detached from my experience. That's when I saw it. Feelings and experience are only a part of my devotional relationship with God. I began to write very quickly, slightly suspecting that God was answering my question.

But I don't feel close to you now.
    That doesn't change the fact that I am.
My emotions toward you are dry.
    Feelings are only a portion. My love transcends any desert. I created the desert, with its beauty. Why would I not be in it? My Holy Spirit does not leave you simply because you cannot feel. If you could feel every aspect of me you would not need faith. Know that in times without feeling, your faith lies in fertile ground, and growth is inevitable if it's your desire.

I sensed I'd been holding God at arm's length, consumed with thoughts about the desert, while he was waiting to welcome me into his embrace if only I'd step into it. But then I shuddered at the sudden thought of a demanding God dictating to me to worship when I didn't feel like it, which brought me full circle. So God, how *do* I quench this dry spirit? The answer was swift and sent me scurrying for my Bible.

Take a drink, my beloved. Take a drink.

And that is what he softly calls out to us in his Word. To me. To you. Take a drink, my beloved! It's so simple we often miss it. Jesus says in John 7:37–38, "If anyone is thirsty, let him come to Me and drink. He who believes in Me, as the Scripture said, 'From his innermost being will flow rivers of living water.'"

Just in case we missed it, he repeats his sweet call. "Blessed are those who hunger and thirst for righteousness, for they shall be satisfied" (Matt. 5:6); "Let the one who is thirsty come" (Rev. 22:17); and "I am the bread of life; he who comes to Me will not hunger, and he who believes in Me will never thirst" (John 6:35). We can go deep into these verses, examining their references to the Holy Spirit, salvation, and Christ alone as the source, but we can also look at them as simply as children, as his call for us to come and believe. And to recognize that we are thirsty in the first place. When the psalmist wrote, "My soul longs for You, as a parched land" in Psalm 143:6, *longs* is the same Hebrew word for *thirsts,* implying craving for water. Do we crave God that much?

I'm a pretty practical person, so as I thought about God's call to "take a drink, my beloved," I asked, *Yes, but how?* Thankfully he answered clearly in Psalm 63, showing me the "how" is as varied as the many ways in which he made us!

It begins, "O God, You are my God; I shall seek You earnestly; my soul thirsts for You, my flesh yearns for You, in a dry and weary land where there is no water." In this psalm about thirsting for God, I saw that I could take a drink just as the psalmist did.

> Thus I have *seen* You in the sanctuary
> To see Your power and Your glory.
> Because Your lovingkindness is better than life,
> My lips will *praise* You.
> So I will *bless* You as long as I live;
> I will *lift up my hands* in Your name.
> My soul is satisfied as with marrow and fatness,
> And my mouth *offers praises* with joyful lips.
> When I *remember* You on my bed,
> I *meditate* on You in the night watches,
> For You have been my help,
> And in the shadow of Your wings I *sing* for joy.
> My soul *clings* to You;
> Your right hand upholds me.
>
> Psalm 63:2–8, emphasis mine

How can we take a drink? Just look at all those verbs. The psalmist beheld God, praised God, blessed God, lifted his hands, offered praises, remembered God, meditated, sang, and clung to God. I can look around at his spectacular creation, see him in it, and praise him. I can get my eyes off of myself and my cursings in the desert and bless him. I can lift my hands and sing in praise, remembering the many things he's done for his people in history and for me in particular. I can meditate on all of these things and cling to him. *That* is a deep drink.

Quenching our dry spirits with that kind of drink brings refreshment beyond comprehension. It ignites the white-hot embers. It causes us to reflect on his character, his goodness, his sovereignty, which then causes us to worship. It also brings us to a place of trust. Like a woman falling in love, either establishing or regaining intimacy, we need to trust the one we love. We must desire to be with him, spend time with him, and know that actions can precipitate feelings. And so we can with Jesus. A good friend of mine once told me that after a lifetime of being a Christian, she actually fell in love with Jesus just two years ago. God brought her to that place through Philip Yancey's book *The Jesus I Never Knew,* and through the video of the Visual Bible's *Book of Matthew* depicting both a Christ who suffered and was crucified but who also laughed and loved children. But mostly, she fell in love with him as she read the Gospels. For two years she read and reread the Gospels until a picture of Jesus emerged from the words into her heart. And she could not help but fall in love with him.

The love and the worship intertwine, and we mustn't wait for emotion to bring us to worship, for it is but a part. Worship is devotion. It causes devotion and is a result of devotion. If you are in a desert, commit yourself to devotion to God and enter into worship with your life. It's far more than what you do on Sunday morning, which incidentally we should enter into with abandon, with at least the same fervor and involvement that we live the most alive part of our lives. In a *Christianity Today* column, Andy Crouch wrote that though he's not opposed to amplified music in worship, he is troubled with something he sees in many contemporary worship services featuring "plugged in" music.

> Next time you're in one of these settings, watch and listen to the congregation. Get ready for the sound of silence. If the sheer volume of amplified worship is like a sonic cathedral, it can also trump the most forbidding medieval liturgy in its capacity to stun churchgoers into a passive stupor. Cynics compare these services to rock concerts, but rock concert audiences participate with a fervor that would put most congregations to shame.[6]

Granted, there are many styles of corporate worship, but let's not offer a lip-locked, unsmiling version at church when we bust loose with friends or at sporting events. Let's ignore the kids behind us kicking our seats, or that crying baby. Let's close our eyes and block out our problems, our jobs, our families, and thoughts of lunch, and give ourselves to God.

Let worship permeate your life. Sing in the car, meditate on his goodness while waiting at the post office, notice that sunset and cool breeze and caterpillar . . . and marvel. Praise him for blazing-red leaves in autumn and lemonade in summer. Do your work as an offering to him and then bask when you feel his pleasure. *Life* can be worship. I've worshiped God in the sweet scent of my newborns and in a broadcast studio when I stopped to smile at his presence and his pleasure. Everyday holiness abounds. It invites a lifestyle of worship.

I think quenching our dryness includes a good bit of waiting on God as well. Andrew Murray writes,

> If our waiting begins by quieting the activities of daily life and being still before God, if we bow and seek to see God in His universal and almighty operation, if we yield to Him in the assurance that He is working and will work in us, if we maintain this place of humility and stillness and surrender until God's Spirit has stirred up in us confidence that He will perfect this work, our waiting will become the strength and joy of our soul.[7]

That waiting is itself a drink. All the ways in which we go to him for a drink cannot help but bring us to the place of worship, of realizing that it's really not about us, it's all about him, which is so very assuring. And we find that place of worship is the bridge that leads us out of the desert, where our thirst is quenched and the flames are fanned in our head-over-heels white-hot love of God.

Moments of worship, of true devotion, are beautiful, leaving footprints across generations. Some years ago, my oldest child, now a college student, was five years old and swinging high in the air on our backyard swing set.

"The mountains are his, the rivers are his, the stars are his handiwork too," she sang. "My God is so great, so strong and so mighty, there's nothing that he cannot do for you. . . ." Over and over she sang. I silently watched her worship as the image of her little toes touching the sky melded into the memory of my own white tennis shoes on five-year-old feet, touching the clouds each time my swing went up. "Jesus loves me this I know . . ." Different song, same worship.

Then another footprint crossed my memory—that of my grandmother Rena Bell Britton. She was a godly woman who excelled at spiritual disciplines and doing but gloried in devotion. The only person she loved more than my grandfather, Floyd, was Jesus. Early one morning, years after my grandfather had gone to live with this first love of hers, she sat at her kitchen table with her hot coffee and open Bible, as was her custom for thousands of days. She and Grandpa had always started each day praying and reading the Bible together, whether they were visiting their seven children across the country or sitting in their yellow kitchen nook under the ceramic praying hands on the wall. She didn't stop just because she now lived alone.

This day, with a kitchen towel across her lap (as was also her custom), she slurped her coffee (never sipped) while her wrinkled hand smoothed the page of the Bible. Thinking her young visitor still asleep, she said softly but audibly to the empty chair next to her, "Well, Floyd, here's our passage for today. Let's see what Jesus has to say. . . ."

And she worshipped the One she loved, ever mindful of the one she missed.

As I remember those footprints of worship, I'm convinced our devotion is God's wellspring for refreshing our dry spirits.

Next, let's look at how we can increase our capacity for growing.

4

I Have My Limits, Right?
Increasing Our Capacity

Everyone loves a morning after a really great sleep, when we bound to the coffeemaker, breathe in the morning air, and think, *Carpe diem!* But let's face it. Some mornings we slug out of bed instead, look into the mirror, and think, *And this is my raw material for today?*

We size up the container of "us" and see our limitations in all their glory. *If only I were smarter, thinner, more energetic, more spiritual, gentler,* we think, then we tack on the afterthought, *And God, I could use a little more PATIENCE!* We know we can grow, but we shake our heads at the small cracked pot God has to work with.

At other times, we are simply complacent. We don't think we need to change or grow in any particular way. Not wanting to rock the boat, we're happy with the status quo.

But wait! What if instead of complacency or frustration with our limitations, we were able to increase our growth potential?

It is possible to increase our capacity to grow when we move from being content with our limitations to wanting more from God and a desire to hold all he has for us—when we trust him as he stretches us, and when we yearn for real growth and the taste of fruit in our lives.

John 15 describes our relationship with Christ in horticultural terms—we are the branches, Jesus is the vine, and the Father is the master gardener. When we stay connected with the gardener, we can trust him more and grow more, even when the growth process becomes messy or painful. But Scripture also uses the metaphor of the potter and the clay. Our heavenly Father is the master potter shaping us, the clay, into beautiful vessels. "But now, O LORD, You are our Father, we are the clay, and You our potter; and all of us are the work of Your hand" (Isa. 64:8). The combination of these two pictures makes a beautiful illustration of us as growing branches and as clay vessels, the vessel holding the growing plant that sometimes needs a repotting by God in order to handle the growth.

Our Pot's Too Small

The pot represents our lives, us as the clay vessel God handcrafts, us as a whole person, body, soul, and spirit. But sometimes we limit our own growth.

- We like the pots we have. We don't want change. ("I'm fine the way I am. This is how God made me.")
- We don't know the gardener well enough to trust him. ("If I let God stretch my limits, what if he makes me go to Africa, or homeschool, or work with 'her'?")

- We don't like the mess of repotting or of cracks in our pots. (Relationships can be messy work. We're afraid that potential pain will shatter us completely or at least beyond repair.)

- We let ourselves get root-bound, alive but growing in circles, limiting our future growth and fruit, never realizing our full capacity. (We serve on the same committee for twenty years out of comfort, not faithfulness. We read the same devotional every morning, year after year after year. We keep to our routine, regardless. We *always* play it safe.)

- We want to stay within the comfort of how we are now and avoid any kind of pruning or splaying, the cutting and spreading of roots for greater growth. ("That class will stretch me beyond reason." "I could give that up, but then what would my life look like without it?")

We understand the idea that he's the potter, that we submit to how he molds us. But I think somewhere along the line we risk falling for the thinking that as adult women, our "pot"—our body, soul, and spirit—is forever one size. That idea is bogus, regarding potted plants *and* who we are. Oh, we may think of our earthen vessels in the three sizes of child, youth, and adult, but where in the world did we get the idea that God just gives us a one-size-fits-all pot once we pass eighteen? We may view some people as having small pots, and those who seem more "spiritual" as having larger pots. After all, how could we dare compare our clay vessels to, say, Billy Graham's or Kay Arthur's or that sweet lady in the front pew who's been evangelizing in laundromats while we silently just wash our socks, trying not to air dirty laundry?

But one day I had a sort of epiphany. I saw myself in this scriptural word picture, stuck at the one-pot-fits-me view. God could basically shape me any way he wanted if I remained pliable, willing, allowing, but I had one basic *size* with certain determined limits. I had a great visual picture of the teaching I'd heard for years that I am God's clay vessel and as I give to others in my life, pouring out myself and the contents of my vessel in love and deeds and service and so on, I must also continue to let God fill me up so I don't run dry. I even understood the concept of staying closely connected to him so he could fill me (with his love, patience, mercy, joy, strength, etc.) to the point that I overflowed. Then I could give to others from God's overflow in my life. Staying filled is good, and giving from overflow is even better, but I always pictured my pot as one size, changing in form and use under his hand but never changing in size. My pot, the body-soul-spirit me with chips and cracks, uniqueness and usefulness, had a certain capacity.

I had my limits, right? My brain wasn't Einstein's, my body wasn't Victoria's Secret, my spirit wasn't that of a giant. I knew I could grow, but the container of me housing the growth had only so much capacity.

Then one day, God shattered my pot, or my concept of it anyway. "Hey, sweetheart," he said (which was nice, since someone else might have said, "Hey, blockhead"), "I always have a bigger pot, and it's only limited by the extent of your growth!" We *are* earthen vessels, cracked pots and all, but we're not static. In the hands of our master potter, we are wet clay that he can shape, change, and *increase in capacity*. He has an unlimited source of clay; he is always ready to reach into his endless storeroom and gift us with whatever size pot our growth requires. Yes, we have limits, but only God truly knows what they are. We look at ourselves in the present, and we see our capability now. We think, *I could never make my body do that. I only have so much brainpower upstairs to work with. I can only handle so much emotionally or I will explode.* And our list of limitations goes on. But God sees beyond those limitations. He sees growth that we think is impossible. Because God is limitless and works within us, we can learn more than we think, we can give more than we think, we can do more than we think, we can love more than we think.

> Then I went down to the potter's house, and there he was, making something on the wheel. But the vessel that he was making of clay was spoiled in the hand of the potter; so he remade it into another vessel, as it pleased the potter to make. Then the word of the LORD came to me saying, "Can I not, O house of Israel, deal with you as this potter does?" declares the LORD. "Behold, like the clay in the potter's hand, so are you in My hand."
>
> Jeremiah 18:3–6

He is capable of making more than one size; he is capable of increasing our capacity for growth.

Here's a similar picture. Leave the plant out for a minute and imagine God filling us like a pitcher of water can fill a small clay pot. God pours into me, and I give out to others. As my pot empties, I go back to the pitcher for a refilling. Now I'm able to give again. Nothing wrong with that, but an increased capacity for growth and giving is better. It looks like this: He fills my pot. I give. I stay right near the source, refilling until I overflow. So now I give from the overflow, and I seek to be filled even more. As the overflow continues, God pours into me and fills me and stretches me, and the growth in my life requires a bigger pot to hold it all. A bigger pitcher to fill my new bigger pot isn't a problem; God is our limitless source, able to fill us and create abundance in our larger pot that continues to overflow. Instead of my one-size-fits-me pot, there's an unlimited supply of nesting clay pots in God's storeroom, waiting. As our capacity increases, we are to delight ourselves in abundance (Isa. 55:2).

The Source of Increased Capacity

We have to be willing to work with the potter and allow him to give us a new pot, to stretch us and increase our ability to hold all he wants to give. When we are willing, he is able. But our willingness isn't the source of more capacity, it's God. He is limitless, and his Spirit, who lives within us, is the endless source that shapes and fills us. All we have is from him: "Every good thing given and every perfect gift is from above, coming down from the Father of lights" (James 1:17).

He is capable of filling us so we can give and to do so to a point of abundance: "And God is able to make all grace abound to you, so that always having all sufficiency in everything, you may have an abundance for every good deed" (2 Cor. 9:8). The Message puts it like this: "God can pour on the blessings in astonishing ways so that you're ready for anything and everything, more than just ready to do what needs to be done."

Many secular writers emphasize growth and moving beyond our limitations with thinking common to the historical period of the Enlightenment, where human potential is emphasized over our weaknesses. Please note I'm not equating increasing our capacity with simple human potential. There is great potential to expand our limitations, but not because of what we bring to the potter's table.

"But we have this treasure in earthen vessels, so that the surpassing greatness of the power will be of God

76

and not from ourselves" (2 Cor. 4:7). "Now to Him who is able to do far more abundantly beyond all that we ask or think, according to the power that works within us" (Eph. 3:20).

Always, always remember the Source that fills us and causes increased capacity in our lives, and the reason he does so: "For it is God who is at work in you, both to will and to work for His good pleasure" (Phil. 2:13). We see our limits, but God sees past them to his purposes. "I can do all things through Him who strengthens me" (Phil. 4:13). All things to which he calls us. Things beyond the current capacity limitations *we* see in our bodies, or minds, or spirits, or emotions.

The Purpose and Power of Greater Capacity

Both our growth and our potential for a greater capacity for growth than we now have, have a powerful purpose. First, a recap on the purpose of our growth. As discussed in the chapter on why we are to think of ourselves as receivers first and givers second, the reason we are to grow is to give. To give from our God-given abundance. Second Corinthians 9:10–11 says, "Now He who supplies seed to the sower and bread for food, will supply and multiply your seed for sowing and increase the harvest of your righteousness; you will be enriched in everything for all liberality, which through us is producing thanksgiving to God." Notice the words *multiply, increase, enrich.* God expanding capacity. As the Message puts it, our generous God is extravagant and "gives you something you can then give away."

Paul held up the example of the Macedonians, who joyfully gave financial gifts even though they were poor. He encourages the Corinthians to give what they can, not what they can't, and he reminds them of the purpose of abundance in the first place. "At this present time your abundance being a supply for their want, that their abundance also may become a supply for your want, that there may be equality" (2 Cor. 8:14). They gave financially, but also "they first gave themselves to the Lord and to us" (v. 5). We are to grow to give and to give from abundance.

Now let's look at the purpose of having an increased capacity. A larger capacity isn't the same thing as growth, it's an increased *ability* to grow, just as we repot a plant in a larger container so it has more room to grow. If a plant's not growing, it doesn't need a bigger pot! But put it in a larger pot with room to expand, and it usually takes off. The purpose of enlarging our capacity is so we have greater growth potential! This results in personal benefits and an increased ability to give, but there's another advantage and purpose as well. As our capacity for growth increases we have more room to *receive*, more room for God to fill us up with more of himself, his strength, his gifts. The result is powerful: gorgeous growth that bears an abundance of fruit in our lives. Fruit that honors him, brings him glory, shines a light in a dark world, and remains. Fruit for God's kingdom that has eternal value.

When We're Ready for a New Pot

God is the one who enlarges us and stretches our capacity, but here are a few things we can keep in mind for our part in the repotting.

1. *Make the paradigm shift.* Move from one-size-fits-all thinking to this: "There is an endless supply of nesting pots ready for my growth." Submitting to the stretching and allowing God to enlarge our capacity can be

a paradigm shift requiring several things: a change or decision to allow God to increase us in a given area, cheerleaders and positive people in our lives, a hard look at the truth over feelings or limitations, and a vice grip on promises from God's Word.

2. *Make choices to increase your capacity.* The first is to believe there is greater capacity in the areas where God desires your present growth. Believe there is an unlimited source to fill it! Believe it by faith, before you feel this, even without feeling this, because God knows no limits in what he can accomplish through us. Second, release negative self-limitations ("I could never . . ."), focusing instead on God's power to do more than we think possible. Third, recognize the strong connection between body, soul, and spirit, and make choices in view of that synergy in order to optimize potential capacity. For example, don't ignore the body and expect growth in the spirit, or ignore your mind, will, or emotions, and expect a healthy body and spiritual life.

3. *Put more in.* We can increase the size of a balloon by putting in more air, and we can increase our tolerance and taste for vegetables by eating more veggies. If you want increased mental capacity, fill the mind. If you want increased capacity physically, put more into the workout. If you want increased ability for hospitality, practice hospitality more often. If you want increased capacity to abide or to worship, put more into it—worship more! Putting more into whatever area we desire growth is our part, an action we can take, but God still causes the growth in his way and through his timing.

Here's an important caveat, however: If we put too much in at one time, we can break our pot. If we stuff a clay pot with the wrong material or with too much force, it can crack, so we must be careful. We humans tend to be doers, to contribute and help God out, so be wise with the input. Sometimes we find our lives overstuffed, and we need to practice saying no to things. Besides, saying no to something often means we can say yes to something better; saying no to that project means we can say yes to a family picnic. We must put in or "do" the right *things* with the right *timing* in the right *amount* and in the right *balance* with the other areas of our lives. That requires seeking God's direction. Prayer is essential.

4. *Stay immersed in the source that fills you.* Think of God pouring into our lives from his bottomless pitcher, filling our pots to overflowing with all that we need until we need bigger pots to hold all that he's pouring into us. Keep your life immersed in his ability to give.

So what does increasing our capacity look like? For example, we don't just want to cram more information into our brains; we want God to increase our capacity to learn. Here are a few examples of increased capacity in the lives of some real women.

Increased Capacity in Real Lives

Increased capacity cannot be better illustrated than in the human body. I ought to know—as I write this, I am eight months pregnant. Since I have a large family you'd think pregnancy would be old hat by now, but I still find myself gasping occasionally at my reflected profile; so much increase, so much elasticity, so much, well, girth. The capacity to house a baby within is simply amazing. When I look at size-four women with their flat tummies (a practice I highly discourage during pregnancy) I marvel that they have the capacity to expand enough to carry eight pounds of living, squirming human inside, then I vacillate between attempting leg lift exercises and giving in to the commercial running through my head: Well, how long has it been since you've had a steaming bowl of Wolf-brand chili?

That God made our bodies capable of such feats is one of the mysteries of the universe. Another is how our bodies are capable of being stretched in strength, suppleness, endurance, and the ability to move beyond current physical limits. Consider marathon runners, professional athletes, Olympic contenders, and moms who manage to get outside and walk or run when it would be so much easier to stay inside and eat chocolate.

Sarah Reinertsen knows about physical limit pushing. She lost her leg at age seven from a tissue disorder but learned to run at age eleven, broke the one-hundred-meter world record for women above-the-knee amputees at age thirteen, and today as an adult holds other records as well. "I still don't know what my limits are," she says. "I'd like to think there aren't any."[1]

God can stretch us physically but also mentally. Barb Larson has not only gained more information than she thought possible, she's seen God expand her mental capacity beyond the limits she once saw. When she and her husband were thirty years old, they arrived in France as English-speaking American missionaries facing twelve months of daunting language study. Barb describes the struggle.

The first day of class the teacher handed each of us a placement test to find out what we knew. After staring at it blankly for a moment I wrote my name at the top and laid down my pen. Understanding, much less two-way communication, seemed unattainable. All I could do was

81

point and gesture during those first few weeks. I dreaded the ring of the telephone because it meant another struggle to understand. The first time we were invited to dinner I nearly fell asleep half way through the evening, exhausted by the mental strain of trying to put together coherent sentences.

But God began to stretch her and increase her ability to learn. She joyfully began to catch hymn numbers and Scripture references in church, and as she laughed at her numerous mistakes she became more comfortable in the learning process. Then, unannounced, Barb said,

The day came when I realized that I could hold a conversation without searching for every word. I could understand, be understood, and even share from my heart. I was building friendships in French. God had stretched my mind and enriched my life in ways I wouldn't have dreamed possible.

The author of *The Art of Thinking* writes, "Most of us never come to know ourselves fully. We see only what we are and never realize the larger part of us: *what we have the capacity to be.*"[2] In the movie *The Kid*, Bruce Willis's character gets the chance to see himself in the future. Amazed, he watches his older self board a plane with the wife and dog he didn't presently have and take off. "I'm a pilot!" he yells. In his present, he didn't imagine that he could become a pilot until he saw into the future. Yet just think . . . God sees our present *and* our future. He sees beyond what we are and fully knows the capacity of what we can become. There is no area of our lives that God is not capable of expanding for his purposes—body, mind, spirit, emotions—any part of us. "You will enlarge my heart" (Ps. 119:32). We just have to be willing to say, "God, I give you me to work with." Then the God who knows no limits can take our limits and increase them into a beautiful form, for he made us capable of being stretched, as moms everywhere have the marks to prove.

There's always a bigger pot, and its size is only limited by the extent of our growth! Before we finish discussing the spirit, let's go a little deeper into the purpose of growing.

5

So How Does My Garden Grow?

Growing with a Purpose

When we grow, it feels wonderful, but what does God say about our growth? What's the point of growing? (Scripture says a thing or two about that.) Growth in the garden of our lives is all about one thing—fruit! And it has a single-minded purpose—to glorify God.

"My Father is glorified by this, that you bear much fruit, and so prove to be My disciples" (John 15:8). We must let that message permeate our beings, our thoughts, our motives, our purpose for wanting growth. We grow to bear fruit so that we glorify him. No matter the beauty resulting in our lives, no matter how others are blessed, no matter what good we do, and no matter the personal benefits we obtain from growing, the primary purpose must always be to glorify God. Please keep that in the forefront of your mind as you read the rest of this book. As we grow our lives *will* be more beautiful, others will be blessed, good will result, and we will reap many personal benefits, but we must always keep the purpose in sight—God's glory.

Not only are we to bear fruit in order to bring glory to God, we are to bear a lot of fruit, much fruit, basketfuls of fruit! It's really not optional. In fact, as people who follow Jesus, we have been chosen to bear fruit.

> "You did not choose Me but I chose you, and appointed you that you would go and bear fruit, and that your fruit would remain, so that whatever you ask of the Father in My name He may give to you."
>
> John 15:16

Now, the promise of being given what we ask for in Christ's name, in order to glorify the Father (John 14:13), is a very exciting thought, but I find it more exciting to know that I was chosen by Jesus to bear fruit. You were too. You and I were selected to bear fruit that will remain, unlike so many other things in our lives that are so easily undone. The empty laundry basket quickly fills again, and a clean kitchen yields to the next meal's mess. When so much of what we do requires doing again, it's downright invigorating to think of lasting things like spiritual fruit. In Romans 7:4 it says we were made to be joined to Christ "that we might bear fruit for God." And when Paul prayed for the Colossian Christians (Col. 2:10), he prayed that they might walk in a manner worthy of the Lord, please him in all respects, and bear fruit in every good work.

Here are a few more things God's Word says about our growth.

- God causes it.

I planted, Apollos watered, but God was causing the growth.

1 Corinthians 3:6

- We are to grow into Christ.

As a result, we are no longer to be children, tossed here and there by waves, and carried about by every wind of doctrine, by the trickery of men, by craftiness in deceitful scheming; but speaking the truth in love, we are to grow up in all aspects into Him, who is the head, even Christ.

Ephesians 4:14–15

- We are to grow in our knowledge of Christ.

But grow in the grace and knowledge of our Lord and Savior Jesus Christ. To Him be the glory, both now and to the day of eternity. Amen.

2 Peter 3:18

- We are to grow in order to give.

That in a great ordeal of affliction their abundance of joy and their deep poverty overflowed in the wealth of their liberality. For I testify that according to their ability, and beyond their ability, they gave of their own accord.

2 Corinthians 8:2–3

And now verse 14:

At this present time your abundance being a supply for their need, so that their abundance also may become a supply for your need, that there may be equality.

A Bit about Growing

I love how the Lord taught profound truth through simple word pictures, often about growing things, as the correlation bears much truth. Since this is a book about our growth as women, let me offer a few relevant observations on plant growth. How do we know that plants are growing? Well, picture a small garden. Imagine a gladiolus perhaps, a fragrant honeysuckle, some colorful zinnias, a blackberry bush, a tomato plant, and a luscious grape arbor. Usually, if these plants are growing, we will observe them changing. They increase in size—get bigger, taller, healthier. They change their form—blossom and become more beautiful. And when the season is right . . . the fruit-bearing plants produce fruit. Some plants grow rapidly, some slowly. Some, like the bulbs, store up energy and potential growth underground, out of sight, ready to grow in the next season. Some plants, after they have blossomed and born fruit, produce seeds, and when the plant has grown to fullness and lived its season, it drops its seeds and dies. But it's a beautiful process, because from this death, the plant gives life as the seed germinates, shoots sprout up, and the new plant grows, eventually yielding beauty, fullness, mature growth, and wonderful fruit. And so can we.

We can know we are growing by looking for some of the same signs of growth we see in plants. When we grow as women in spirit, body, or soul, we will be able to observe change in our lives. Strengths and skills and wisdom will increase. We will become healthier, more beautiful. We will change form; we will not always be as we are now, and that's a very exciting thought. Sometimes we'll grow rapidly, sometimes slowly, and sometimes, like an underground bulb, the growth will be stored up, waiting for another season before we can observe change. And the most beautiful part is that as we blossom as women, bursting forth with the beauty and fragrance that God has known was in us from the day we were created, fruit emerges in our lives. Fruit that blesses those around us and glorifies our God.

So what does that growth look like in our lives, practically speaking? Like this:

- We've changed for the better. Bad habits have been stopped. New good habits have begun.
- Thinking patterns have changed from negative to positive.
- We've acquired wisdom, maturity, or knowledge.
- We've contributed to someone or something.
- We've added to or increased our "raw materials" as we've learned new principles, skills, talents, information, interests.
- We've added productivity.
- We are better people in character than we were before.
- We are more like Christ.
- We have more spiritual fruit; we are more loving, joyful, peaceful, patient, kind, gentle, and self-controlled, to name a few things.

Ideally our lives will become like a beautiful plant, growing in fullness, mature growth, and wonderful fruit. Then after just the right number of ordained seasons of beautiful springs, lush summers, and abundant fall harvests, we will enter the winter of our lives and see our seed, our precious children or others we've influenced, continue the cycle of growth and fruit bearing, bringing honor to God.

Throughout this book we'll look at ways we can grow that reflect the definition of growth. We want to mature, increase in complexity and influence, and experience progressive development; we can spring up and grow in our place or situation throughout our whole person—growth in our physical being, our spiritual being, and in the depth of our souls. But let's set the record straight first. I am not advocating growth for growth's sake. I don't want to add to the number of self-help books that focus on growth as the goal, with whatever spiritual emphasis that seems right to them in the world of relativism. Mere growth is not the goal. Let me illustrate with a little story.

Once upon a time, in a land far away and very hot (called Texas), there grew a garden. And in this garden were all kinds of delicious things to eat. But the most amazing thing of all was the okra trees. They grew tall and lush . . . just like in that other story about Jack and his beanstalk, only not quite as tall and minus the giant. All the gardens in the land grew okra as well, but they didn't have okra trees. They had the normal variety that grew, well, shorter. The gardener was so proud.

"Look at my beautiful okra," he said, beaming. The stalks were tall, the branches were many, and the leaves were large and lush. One evening, with great anticipation of their delicious dinner, the gardener's wife heated her cast-iron skillet with oil, set out the cornmeal and salt and pepper, and took the largest basket she had with her into the garden to harvest their crop. But alas, when she lifted the abundant foliage, to her dismay she found . . . well, not much.

She looked harder for her expected bounty, but the okra was few and far between the branches, and it was very, very small, rather like little cocktail wieners. Amidst all those giant okra trees, only a smidgen of teeny, weeny okra could be found. So the gardener's wife dried her tears, called her husband, and they headed out to eat. The moral of the story? Abundant growth doesn't necessarily mean a full skillet.

In the words of Dave Barry, I am not making that up. Our little Texas garden that year yielded tree-sized plants with anemic-sized okra because we allowed rampant growth when we should have pruned. Since then, we've learned a wee bit about growing things; sometimes we have to get out the garden shears.

Pruning and Abiding for a Miracle Grow Crop

As we learn more about growth and understand its purpose in our lives, recognize its signs, internalize the reasons, and dedicate ourselves to it, we would be wise to remember the message in John 15 about pruning and abiding. Without these two gardening essentials there may be growth, but there will be little fruit. And so it is with grapes, which Bruce Wilkinson explains well in *Secrets of the Vine*.

> Left to itself, a grape plant will always favor new growth over more grapes. The result? From a distance, luxurious growth, an impressive achievement. Up close, an underwhelming harvest. That's why the vinedresser cuts away unnecessary shoots, no matter how vigorous, because a vineyard's only purpose is . . . grapes.[1]

He also explains how, horticulturally speaking, growers will prune their vineyards more intensively as the vines age. Why? Because every year the vine has a greater capacity for growth, and without pruning, it will weaken and produce less fruit.

And so it is with us. Every year as we mature, we have a greater capacity for growth as well, so if we are producing any fruit at all, the Father will prune us to produce even more fruit.

"I am the true vine, and My Father is the vinedresser. Every branch in Me that does not bear fruit, He takes away; and every branch that bears fruit, He prunes it so that it may bear more fruit" (John 15:1–2). That's painful sometimes, but filled with hope and promise. Under God's shears, growing women move from potential to producing, from some fruit to abundant fruit. Our Master Gardener prunes us in so many ways, with methods unique to who he made us to be and the type of fruit he's producing in us. Pruning is far from "one size fits all"; it can be the severing or cutting back of things that keep us from our greater priorities, things of temporal value, good things that are not best, or things (even valuable things) that shift our focus from that which God desires of us at that time.

John 15 is my favorite passage of Scripture. Jesus paints the vivid picture of a fruit-bearing vine, not only emphasizing the often-painful pruning required, but also the sweetness of abiding in him.

> "Abide in Me, and I in you. As the branch cannot bear fruit of itself unless it abides in the vine, so neither can you unless you abide in Me. I am the vine, you are the branches; he who abides in Me and I in him, he bears much fruit, for apart from Me you can do nothing."
>
> John 15:4–5

Wilkinson well states the importance of abiding—having a connected relationship to Jesus—in our growth.

> If we are not abiding, we wither and die and become of no spiritual use. If you stay connected to Him, if you draw spiritual nourishment from Him, if you allow the power that flows through Him to flow through you, nothing will hold you back from reaching the most abundant life possible.[2]

I love this visual image of a growing vine: a very old, sturdy vine's trunk, flowing with nutrient-filled sap, and a vigorous branch attached securely to the trunk, taking in all that it needs. But instead of a uniform-sized connection of all the branches, some connections are larger than others.

> The only limitation on the amount of sap that goes to the fruit is the circumference of the branch where it meets the vine. That means that the branch with the largest, least-obstructed connection with the vine is abiding the most and will have the greatest potential for a huge crop.[3]

That picture beautifully illustrates how we can grow in our ability to abide in Jesus, increase our connection of being with him. Abiding is all about being *with* the person of Jesus. The flurry of "doing" is calmly absent in this branch-in-vine word picture. We can increase our depth of being *with* him and aim for the least-obstructed connection possible. The Lord taught me this, again, not long ago.

My morning prayer time had been filled with the usual: praise, thanksgiving, and lots of requests for needs in my life and others. During the busy day I'd continued to dialogue with God. But later that night, as I prayed I suddenly heard myself. "Lord, please direct me as I . . . keep me walking where you'd have me to . . ." and so on. I was struck with how often I focused my prayers on staying in his will, making the right choices, doing what he wanted. That night his Spirit stopped me. He wanted me to quit concentrating on being in his will and focus on the joy of simply being with him. It was as if he said, "Child, relax. You *are* in my will. Would you please just enjoy me?"

I got out of bed and went to my bookshelf, sensing there was something God wanted me to read. Immediately my eyes fell on one book I'd had for a long time but had never read, John Piper's *Desiring God.* I got back into bed and was amazed at what I read in the first sentence of the introduction:

> You might turn the world on its head by changing one word in your creed. The old tradition says,
>
>
>
> The chief end of man is to glorify God
>
> AND
>
> Enjoy him forever.
>
>
>
> "And"? Like ham and eggs? Sometimes you glorify God and sometimes you enjoy him? Sometimes he gets glory, sometimes you get joy? "And" is a very ambiguous word! . . . This book aims to persuade you that
>
>
>
> The chief end of man is to glorify God
>
> BY
>
> Enjoying him forever.[4]
>
>

I was moved that God cared enough about my state of abiding with him that he led me to a specific book that night and spoke to me in my prayers. "Abide in me, and I in you. You'll enjoy it immensely."

Pruning and abiding are deep subjects, delightful to study at length. I invite you to dive into a study of John 15, even if it's familiar territory. *Secrets of the Vine* is terrific on the subject; it's a quick read with great depth and insight. When we allow God to prune as he sees fit, and we learn to delight in abiding in him, we will grow in a way that he loves and planned for us—we'll have *lasting* fruit in our lives.

Reasons to Grow

Why should we want to grow? What's the purpose? Consider these reasons:

- to bear fruit
- for his glory
- to give
- to live to your full potential of whom God made you to be
- to accomplish all the kingdom purposes God has for you
- to experience life abundantly
- to be a reflection of him, reflecting his glory
- to be a light to a dark world
- to keep the whole person in shape (body, soul, and spirit) so we are ready to be of service to our commander in chief

Jeremiah 31:12 says, "And their life will be like a watered garden." I see that garden. It's the one that's been in my visions for many years. It's sunny. It's enclosed with a white picket fence with a white arched arbor covered in climbing roses. Inside there are colorful flowers, delightfully fragrant herbs, useful and delicious vegetables. There's a bench for pondering, and a little garden sculpture tucked where you don't expect it, whimsical and surprising. And when my garden is watered, it sparkles in freshness. It's nourished and refreshed and . . . it grows; it produces beauty for the eyes and nourishment for the body. And it deeply nourishes my soul. It's a place for the soul to just be. I long to make such a garden. Can't you just see it?

Yet God says my *life* shall be like a watered garden! Imagine, my life, your life—sunny, colorful, delightfully fragrant, useful, pondering, surprising, sparkling, fresh, nourishing, refreshed . . . and growing!

Now, let's move from talking about the spirit to the next section, the body.

Part 2

Going South by the Scenic Route

The Body

6

Chocolate or Nachos and Other Nutritional Quandaries
Fueling and Nurturing

S o what's your pleasure—chocolate or nachos? Do you savor the sweet or do you like a little kick to your taste buds? Have you ever read "One third less fat!" on a food label and wondered, *Less than what? A bowl of lard?* Ah, such nutritional quandaries. Do you drink what you should, eat what you should, and refrain when you should . . . most of the time? Don't quit reading! There's room to grow in wisdom and knowledge about what we put into our bodies without becoming catatonic at the thought of banishing sweets—or jalapenos, for that matter. Keep your chocolate, keep your nachos, but do consider your water intake, fasting, eating for good health, and the nurturing you can create in your kitchen. Why? Because taking care of our physical bodies is so important in the effort to keep Mama from going south, and our physical health impacts our mental, emotional, and spiritual health as well.

Water, Water Everywhere, but Not a Drop to Drink

When I was in college I developed the very bad habit of starting my day with coffee, switching to Cokes around lunch, then drinking tea for dinner. It was caffeine from sunrise to sunset. The only use I had for water was in the shower and also right after my morning run, when I'd manage a glass. It was years before I saw the dichotomy of trying to be healthy by running while consuming only caffeine-laden beverages. In college I never thought about the need to drink water. A few years later I tried to drink more of it, but rationalized that lots of caffeine wasn't hurting me and I needed the morning and afternoon pick-me-up. Thankfully, over time, I've learned to hydrate my body. Water is an essential life-giving ingredient to health, one we cannot do without.

Water is the beverage of choice, or at least it should be. It's the only thing we can drink that doesn't require our body to work to process, so other beverages don't count in our daily water intake. All living things are mostly made up of water, including our tissues, cells, and fluids, and all of our body systems need it to function, including our circulatory, urinary, and digestive systems. Think of it as our body's transportation system. Water delivers nutrients throughout our bodies and carries toxins and waste products out, two crucial activities for health. We lose water every day through perspiration, elimination, and breathing, so we must replace it. Like most people, I'd certainly heard that I needed to drink eight glasses of water a day, but knowledge didn't lead to lifestyle change until I took to heart the impact of not drinking it—illness. Little water intake means we have a higher concentration of waste products and dead cells in our blood, and those toxins floating in our bloodstream lead to disease. "Body tissue is poisonous once it is dead and dead cells must be removed. When we drink plenty of pure water the poisonous wastes are flushed out of the system."[1] Realizing that and imagining the toxins running through my poorly hydrated blood is what made me change and begin to drink more water. It's the ticket for clean blood and a healthy body.

So how much water do *you* drink? Chances are you know you need eight glasses a day, but are you drinking that much? Naively I used to wonder which glasses the recommendation meant. My mom's little juice glasses or my big tumblers that held a whole can of soda? Neither. We need eight eight-ounce glasses of water a day, or sixty-four ounces. So forget the glass thing and just remember that we need sixty-four ounces, or two quarts, of pure water every day.

How to Get It Down

Thirst alone will not tell you how much you need to drink. In fact, I never used to be thirsty. Here's the key for getting the right amount: You *have* to measure it! Especially at the beginning. And it isn't a big deal. Here are two simple ways to make sure you are getting enough water each day. In her book *Greater Health God's Way* Stormie Omartian recommends drinking sixteen ounces four times a day, thirty to forty-five minutes before breakfast, lunch, dinner, and bedtime. Then you only have to think about it four times a day. I don't even want to think about it that many times, so I have several quart containers that I use. Sometimes I grab my quart mason jar and fill it in the morning, refilling it once during the day. By bedtime I've had my two-quart requirement. I used this method a lot at first because the wide mouth of the jar allowed me to float sliced lemon in it. It made the flavor a bit more palatable and was pretty too. Now I usually use a plastic one-quart or one-liter water bottle, and I make sure I drink about two of those before bed. I can sip on it throughout the day, and with the cap closed it's always ready to take with me when I leave the house. It fits perfectly in my car cup holder and curbs my desire to swing through a drive-through for a Coke. I'm no purist claiming that nothing but water ever passes my lips, but I have radically changed my lifestyle from coffee-coke-tea only to include sixty-four ounces of water each day for better health, softer skin, and a better complexion.

Fasting

Eating whole foods and avoiding bad ones is a good goal, but what about specifically not eating, or fasting? You may wonder how that could possibly be part of your growth plan. I've been a Christian since I was a child, but frankly, fasting wasn't something I thought much about as a young adult. It seemed an archaic, radical, Old Testament thing to do. Then one day my husband and I faced a dilemma that could only be fought in the spiritual realm. Someone I loved had become involved in the occult. I'd never read anything about fasting other than the occasional Scripture passage I'd come across and had never heard it talked about much, but the Holy Spirit suddenly laid upon my heart the desire to fast. As I did, I was amazed at the depth and clarity of my prayer life. I began to understand why God says some things are only possible by prayer *and* fasting. My husband and I were in a spiritual battle with a life at stake, and fighting the battle brought attacks from the enemy in our own home. Fasting girded up my armor, strengthened my fortress, fought fear, and focused my prayers. It was also simply an act of obedience. God had directed it.

Since then I've fasted with some regularity with my husband and our church. It has definitely been a part of my growth as a woman and a Christian, and I know God has much to teach me in this realm. I don't write about this as an expert, but as a fellow journeyman with you.

There's much to be learned on the topic, so I recommend you read more about it. Here's a quick overview. Fasting is mentioned in both the Old and New Testaments, some eighty times in all. It was practiced by Jesus and recommended by him. In Matthew 6:16 he says, "When you fast . . ." Not if. *When.* I'm discussing it in the body section of this book, but I could have put it in the spirit section, since it's a spiritual discipline. Fasting is all about denying our selves, and it's good for the spirit, body, and soul. It's an act of obedience to be done for his glory, and God just may use it as a tool to keep you from going south. Here's why.

Spiritual and Physical Benefits

Some spiritual benefits and reasons to fast include praying for something specific in your life, weakening the power of the flesh, gaining spiritual strength, making an offering to God, giving attention to your inner man instead of your physical body, hearing God better or seeking his direction, battling the enemy, gaining freedom or healing, and cleansing the heart.

In *The Cost of Discipleship,* Dietrich Bonhoeffer wrote about the spiritual implications of fasting:

> Jesus takes it for granted that his disciples will observe the pious custom of fasting. (Refer to Matt. 6:16–18.) Strict exercise of self-control is an essential feature of the Christian's life. Such customs have only one purpose—to make the disciples more ready and cheerful to accomplish those things which God would have done. Fasting helps to discipline the self-indulgent and slothful will which is so reluctant to serve the Lord, and it helps to humiliate and chasten the flesh. By practicing abstemiousness we show the world how different the Christian life is from its own. If there is no element of asceticism in our lives, if we give free rein to the desires of the flesh (taking care of course to keep within the limits of what seems permissible to the world), we shall find it hard to train for the service of Christ. When the flesh is satisfied it is hard to pray with cheerfulness or to devote oneself to a life of service which calls for much self-renunciation.[2]

Fasting has physical benefits as well. It brings clearer thinking, breaks bad eating habits, adds strength and energy (after the fast), helps with self-control, fights stress and depression, gives our bodies a break from the work of digesting food, cleanses and purges toxins, and can help control weight. I believe the spiritual benefits far outweigh the physical, and that should be our motivation as Christians, but God gave us a physical body and allows the physical benefits of fasting to strengthen our whole person as well. We can enjoy this gift!

A Simple Fast

The first thing to do is decide how long you want to fast. This is not an "until I collapse" event. Deciding the length ahead of time is best. Eat especially healthy for several days beforehand, and if you drink bottled water, have all the water you'll need for the fast on hand. You don't need to be in a grocery store during your fast. A good place to begin is with a twenty-four-hour fast. I used to think this meant I could not eat at all that day. Including the night before, that amounts to a thirty-six-hour fast. Instead, I learned from Stormie Omartian that a twenty-four-hour fast means you stop eating after dinner at 6:00 P.M., skip breakfast and lunch the next day, drinking only water, and break the fast that night after 6:00 P.M. with a light dinner such as a steamed vegetable with a fruit or vegetable salad or baked potato. This was an easy way for me to begin, because I thought, *I only have to miss two meals.* You can extend the fast to thirty-six-hours by skipping dinner the second night as well and breaking your fast the next morning with fruit, followed by a light lunch (salad and plain baked potato for example).

Many people recommend fasting regularly each week, with longer fasts a couple of times a year or as God directs you. I found that a twenty-four-hour fast beginning after dinner Sunday night and breaking it with a light dinner Monday night worked well. This is an excellent spiritual discipline. As I write this, I am expecting a child and cannot fast, and although I was never legalistic about it, it is a spiritual discipline I miss and look forward to resuming, even semiregularly.

Here are a few fasting tips:

1. Who should *not* fast: pregnant and nursing women, hypoglycemics, diabetics, or those with any serious physical condition or illness. If in doubt, ask your doctor. Also, I would advise you not to fast if you struggle in any way with an eating disorder. Millions

of women suffer from anorexia nervosa and bulimia; if you are among them, you do not need to complicate the issue of food and faith, you need loving support and medical help.

2. How you break the fast is important:
    Resume eating with raw or lightly steamed veggies and fruits.
    No junk food!
    Never overeat afterward.
    Avoid meat, dairy, and fats initially.
3. Exercise lightly while fasting, not strenuously.
4. Do not drink alcohol, tea, coffee, or soft drinks while fasting.
5. Remember that headaches are common, since your body is releasing impurities.
6. Weakness and dizziness are common too.
7. If you are very weak but want to continue the fast, add a homemade vegetable broth to drink. Just boil a potato, an onion, carrots, and celery for an hour, then strain and drink.
8. Remember that it gets easier the more you do it.

Food

Perfectly grilled salmon fillets, Mediterranean rice pilaf, asparagus tips with garlic butter and artichoke hearts, and crème brûlée topped with kiwi and raspberries for dessert. Lovely. Or how about lobster bisque, lean prime rib, grilled seasonal vegetables, and a Caesar salad. Hearty but chic. And then there's always fried chicken, mashed potatoes and gravy, fried okra, and yeast rolls for all my Southern sisters. Have I mentioned banana pudding yet? Even the thought of a crisp apple with a slice of fresh cheese can make our mouths water and send us heading for the kitchen. Isn't it wonderful God gave us such a smorgasbord of flavors, colors, textures, and variety to sustain our bodies with nutrients and delight our taste buds at the same time? He could have just made beige nutrient wafers for sustenance, or he could have left off the taste buds during creation, but no, in his great creativity he allowed food to fuel us while also satisfying on a number of levels. Nutrition and nurturing in one package. What a gift.

Yet it is a gift that comes with some responsibility. Food must be kept in proper perspective and used as God intended, not given greater importance than its purpose. A New Zealand Masters runner and author, Roger Robinson, said, "The experts are always telling us to 'listen to your body.' If I listened to my body, I'd live on toffee bars and port wine. Don't tell me to listen to my body—it's trying to turn me into a blob."[3]

Food has the power to give life or bring death. You may think, *I know how to eat, I know how to feed my family, I know what I like to cook. What's to learn?* Well, plenty. A shortcut for Mama to go south quickly (and take the family with her) is to be undernourished or, more commonly, overfed (the biblical word for that is gluttony) or comfortable with the thought that Krispy Kreme donuts and chocolate milk each morning is a well-rounded meal. It's well-rounded all right . . . on our thighs.

But what and how we eat is more important than its relationship to how we fit into our jeans. We want to be women who are healthy and fit from the inside out with enough energy and stamina to carry out our calling, and who responsibly nourish our families as well. We increase our capacity to stay north when we decide there are more ways to grow in the area of food—besides our girth. I'm not a nutritionist or health food purist (you will see me at the Sonic drive-in occasionally), but I'm thankful that I've

107

grown in nutritional knowledge. I've actually been able to shake my Southern urge to slather everything in fat and throw it in a cast-iron skillet. It also helps to have friends who know more about nutrition than I do (they never eat at Sonic but love me anyway).

Dishing Up Nutrients

While far from a nutritional manual, these few basics on healthy eating will keep Mama and the family from going south, and will also increase our health, help us avoid illness, and properly fuel our bodies.

Many, many diseases of our day are strongly associated with what we put into our mouths. When we discuss nutrition, we will find that God's Word contains enduring, time-tested, and scientifically established principles that, if followed, can greatly reduce sicknesses that are due to physical causes.[4]

Lose the word diet *from your vocabulary*. Replace that restrictive and often unhealthy dieting mentality with simple, healthful eating habits (and pure water and exercise) as a lifestyle. It's what you eat as the norm that counts. We shouldn't diet to get to X pounds then Katie-bar-the-door after reaching our goal. Nor does healthy eating mean that indulging in a piece of cheesecake is a mortal sin.

Keep it simple and include variety. The subject of nutrition can be overwhelming, with *much* disagreement and contradiction among the experts, so to make good nutrition possible for you and your family, start with just one or two things you want to change and keep your eating plan, menus, and recipes simple.

Try to eat food as close to how God made it as possible. Whole, living, natural, unprocessed, "real" food. The farther food gets from how it began, the more destructive it is for our bodies. Aim for fewer processed foods in the shopping cart by buying more from the perimeter of the store; the outer aisles of a store are where you usually find the produce, meats, breads, and dairy, while "food in boxes" are usually located in the interior aisles. Processing does allow foods to be shipped and stored longer and offers convenience, but it strips the life right out of the food. All the while they fool us by throwing in a few vitamins and minerals, which is nothing compared to what they took out, and then add chemicals, preservatives, and colorings. They call that "enriched."

Eat as much plant food as you can. "Plant food, the basis for man's diet since the Garden of Eden, is a gold mine of good, nontoxic nutrition. Loaded with vitamins, minerals, enzymes, and cancer-fighting phytochemicals, these foods must be the foundation for a healthy diet."[5] What and how much? Fruit and veggies—as many as possible, some raw, steamed, fresh if possible, then frozen and canned as a last resort. Minimums—fruit (two to three fresh raw servings), vegetables (four to six half cup servings, half of them raw if possible), whole grains (six-plus bread, cereal, rice, pasta), legumes (one, beans and peas), and nuts. Start early in the day to get the fruit and veggies in and use them for snacks, otherwise it's hard to get them all in during the day. Another suggestion is to think of your plate in percentages. Make it 50 percent fruits/veggies, 25 percent whole grains/starch, and 25 percent meat, fish, or poultry.[6] Or to help you initially, you might want to keep a simple record to track your progress in eating the required minimums by making a worksheet listing the food categories and how many servings you should have (i.e., fruits 1, 2, 3; veggies 1, 2, 3, 4).[7] Simply cross off a number from the food group as you eat it. This is far easier than a food diary or a complicated, time-consuming menu, and it's gratifying to see your healthy accomplishments at the end of the week. If all that sounds like too much work, simply go back to the heading of this paragraph and just eat as much plant food as you can.

Eat only what you need. In other words, avoid the sin of gluttony.

Limit or avoid fried foods, sugar, chemicals (artificial sweeteners and MSG for starters), high-fat foods (with hydrogenated oils and saturated fats), large amounts of red meat, highly processed meat products like hot dogs, bologna, and salami.

Make healthy substitutions. Replace white sugar with raw unprocessed honey, pure maple syrup, blackstrap molasses, fruit, or fruit juice. Replace margarine, hydrogenated oils, and saturated fats with olive oil and real butter in moderation. Substitute brown rice for white rice and natural peanut butter for commercially processed brands (the commercial ones may be creamy, but it is really peanuts and large amounts of shortening). Replace white flour and its products with whole grains as often as possible. Look for "stone ground" on the label, since plain wheat bread and wheat flour have a lot of white flour in them that has been stripped of most nutritional value. Gradually introduce some whole-grain pastas to your family or try some of the new blended pasta with both regular and whole grains. Another great thing you can do for yourself and your family is to try freshly ground flour. The reason white flour has been stripped of all its nutrition is that those are the elements that go rancid within seventy-two hours of milling—so after these elements have been refined out, the flour can be shipped and stored on grocers' shelves. But in the process, we've lost everything that was good about it.

I don't make all of these replacements religiously. I have both plain and whole-wheat pastas in my pantry, and I still enjoy making chocolate chip cookies for my children, but I've learned to make lots of healthy substitutions. This can add life to our diets and years to our lives. I look forward to continued growth and improvement in nutrition. I will continue to read, talk to friends who are ahead of me in this area, attend nutritional seminars on subjects like cooking with whole grains, and listen to tapes. I'd even like to take a cooking class. Learning and trying new things, and even changing some bad habits, takes effort, but the effort will result in invigorating growth. Growth that benefits our families and us. After all, if we are the primary meal planner and grocery shopper in our homes, we hold the nutritional key for our families' health. When trying to make changes, remember this: Set the example by *modeling* healthy eating as the norm, set specific goals ("four veggies a day" instead of "try to eat better"), and take small steps.

According to Hippocrates, "A wise man should consider that health is the greatest of human blessings," and that you should "let your medicine be your food, and your food your medicine."

Dishing Up Nurturing

Food doesn't just meet our nutritional needs, it nurtures us. Last week my nine-year-old daughter Allison played one of her favorite games, "A's Café," where she is the sole proprietor, chef, and waitress. She told me the daily special, wrote down my order, prepared it with stylish presentation, served it, and brought me my bill. I munched on my chicken salad surrounded with strawberries, kiwi, and banana slices, and contemplated my colorful luncheon

111

feast and the powerful role of food, both nutritionally and as a nurturing component. I was filled and nourished physically, but playing A's Café with Allison also filled her cup as we pretended together. It reached that intangible that food often evokes—the power to touch body and soul.

Kitchen Moments for Children

My mother was an expert at nourishing and nurturing through food. I still remember her crust-free sandwiches and chicken noodle soup that were always waiting for me on snowy Milwaukee days when I walked home for lunch. I didn't walk home just to eat. I walked in the door anticipating my mother's love, which she always supplied as plentifully as she did the noodles in my bowl. She used her skill and art in the kitchen to create tangible expressions of love for us. Her cherry surprise pie wasn't just a dessert, it was a gift given with more heart than a Macy's gift wrapped with a french silk bow. During peanut butter cookie baking sessions, she'd roll out the balls of dough in her hands and let me dip the fork lightly in flour and press crisscross imprints in the cookies, which also left an indelible imprint in my memory. Dip. Crisscross. "How's that, Mama?" "Beautiful." Dip. Crisscross. "A little less flour, honey." Dip. Crisscross. "Better. These are your Dad's favorite, you know."

My mother's time in the kitchen was an extension of her love for us. Art, skill, and time melded into edible expressions of caring, food used as a tool for loving, no strings attached. Sadly I think we've lost so much of that in my generation. When my older girls were small, I remember reading them a children's book illustrating this. The beginning of the book showed an old-fashioned kitchen with kids in overalls holding bushels of fruit and wearing berry stains on their mouths. The mom rolled out dough, and they made a pie from the fruit they'd picked. Then it showed a slightly more modern kitchen with a pie baking and canned fruit containers on the counter. Toward the end of the book it showed a modern kitchen with Mom's briefcase in the corner, the frozen pie box in the trash, and the pie in the microwave. I've forgotten if the message of the book was the loss of an era or the empowerment of women. Either way, it saddened me as I thought of my frozen boxes in the trash, a testament to my generation's convenience and liberation, a crumpled contrast to the gifts of the heart that were created in my mother's kitchen. And her mother's before her. After that, I started making a few more pies and cakes from scratch with my daughters.

I remember one of my aunts once said, "I need to encourage my daughter to make cookies with her daughter. She seldom does that, and it's important." Reflecting on thirty-plus years of memories, I know what she means. Though I'll never be able to make a from-scratch piecrust as good as my mom's, creating in the kitchen with my children touches me in secret places. Who knows what delicious memory or feeling will be released in them thirty years from now by an unexpected scent, a familiar taste, or a long-forgotten photograph capturing kitchen moments of crafting love? Kitchen moments expressing love through the nurturing aspect of planning, cooking, and serving food are worth the effort. Like my feast from A's Café, we can use food as a tool to express and enhance our walk in the spirit of love, joy, and peace, providing memories, traditions, comfort.

Go ahead. Keep a couple of frozen pies in your freezer, but dust off a recipe and plan a kitchen moment with a child you love or a kitchen gift for a person who needs a tangible expression of caring. Martha Stewart may have truckloads of detractors, but lots of people are drawn to her brand of living for various reasons. I'll never do (or want to do) half the things she does, but I applaud the rise in respectability and attention she's given to the domestic arts. I occasionally watch her show with my girls, and sometimes they are inspired to go create something. And I'm inspired by the memories of my mother and aunts, whom I watched iron a shirt perfectly, fold a towel just so, and make delicious things in the kitchen from scratch (without the aid of a TV show).

Celebrate Life with Food

Food is often a backdrop in the drama of life, accentuating so much that is rich and fulfilling in our souls. It is often the accompaniment to our expressions of love, joy, peace, comfort, traditions, hospitality, and memory-making. I still remember the Caesar salad tossed at our table as prelude to a perfect meal, underscored with soft music the night my husband dropped to one knee with a velvet box. On one anniversary we chased escapee live lobsters before they became the dinner celebration of our love. When my son was born, my best friend showed up at my bedside with her version of the world's most perfect hamburger. Joy and food are quintessential partners.

The joy of friendship will never be forgotten in the memory of our friend Ron Nelson coming to our door unexpectedly one night with a formal invitation rolled up with ribbon requesting "the pleasure of our company" at a formal dinner for four in his and Nancy's home. Despite a pouring rain, he delivered the invitation in a tuxedo. And just last week we celebrated the joy of our first child's eighteenth birthday and graduation from high school with a big party and lots of food. Creating the various food tables,

114

making seventy-five chicken kabobs, and cooking all day was half the fun.

Peace and comfort are often found in food, like on the night of my mother's death when my neighbor Lois Ash arrived with enough food for an army, knowing my house was filling with people. I hadn't eaten decently in days, and I still remember the comfort I found in her gift of glazed ham and fresh green beans with onions like my grandmother used to make.

Traditions nearly always feature food from holiday menus. I think of Tim making caramel apples with the children in the fall, and my tradition of making Martha Washington candy at Christmas with my stepsister Donna, as well as my family's weekly habit of grilling out every Saturday night.

I love to incorporate great things to eat into memory-making adventures, like the brisket in a basket picnic when we dedicated the land we'd just bought to the Lord. Another memory is the all-day, wrecked-kitchen, I've-never-seen-bigger-pots-in-my-life homemade tamale making with my friend Brenda Koinis. And one of my favorites was the summer day we made "watermelons" with the kids and their friends out of lime, lemon, and raspberry sherbet with chocolate chips for seeds. You must have countless examples as well.

Hospitality

Hospitality is seldom practiced without food (and *never* without food in the South, even if it's just a glass of iced tea and an Oreo). My friend Janie Hodgkins is known for her tea parties. When she says, "Why don't you drop over for tea?" you can expect a treat: a tea table with lace linens and pretty pots, scones with cream, chocolates, candied fruits, and other goodies, most of which she keeps in her freezer for tea parties put together in a flash. Sharing blessings and desiring to spend time with other people are what hospitality is all about, regardless of how the table is set or what is served. After a recent move and time of unsettledness, my family and I are thoroughly enjoying being able to practice hospitality again and the relationship building that it brings.

Simple Ways to Make Kitchen Nurturing Happen

Using food to share kitchen moments with children, highlight important moments in our lives, and practice hospitality takes time. It also takes planning, shopping, and usually effort, but the effort is worth it when we provide nutrients *and* nurturing. A willing heart is the greatest asset. In a world of fast-food restaurants, packaged convenience foods, and restaurant dining, kitchen nurturing stands out. Get to know your family's favorites, create food traditions, stock your pantry and freezer with easy-to-make items. Buy old baskets and plates at garage sales and store with ribbon, jars, raffia, and tags to create a "welcome," "moving in," or "new baby" food basket. I still remember one dinner in a basket my friend gave me years ago just because she knew I was busy and overwhelmed one day. A great resource is my friend Jane Jarrell's book *Love You Can Touch: Gift Ideas That Show You Care.*

Don't be afraid to use your best things for your family. Don't wait for Christmas to bring out the china and cloth napkins. Surprise your family and vary the location of a meal occasionally. Plan picnics! Refresh your mind-set from one of drudgery to one of joy found in meeting the needs of your family. Delight in that well-stocked, well-organized pantry, those meals you bulk-cooked and have waiting in the freezer, that special meal you've planned. It's an expression of your creativity and love, a great place to grow as a woman. (Just keep the pizza delivery number handy too!)

Drinking pure water, learning about fasting, increasing our nutritional knowledge, and taking the effort to nurture through food affect our bodies physically, but they also have carryover value to our spirit and soul lives. Growing in these areas will affect our whole person and keep our families from going south too.

Those are some ideas for taking care of the *inside* of our bodies; next let's look at the *outside*.

7

Did Sleeping Beauty Exercise?

Energizing Our Bodies

H ow much happiness is gained, and how much mis-
ery escaped by frequent and violent agitation of the
body," writes Dr. Johnson in *Jim Fixx's 2nd Book of
Running*. Unconvinced? Perhaps your exercise philosophy
is closer to that of the following bit of fiction.

Mary-Margaret stretched the phone cord across the counter
and pushed her bar stool back far enough to allow her to prop
her feet up on the ceramic poodle, which also gave her more
tummy space between her stool and the counter. She absent-
mindedly drummed her red manicured nails on her iced-tea
glass while she chatted, enjoying her leisurely morning. Her
eyes grew wide in response to her friend's question.

"A stop at the gym? As in, to exercise? Now, why in the world would I want to do that? Have you been drinking? The last time I visited the gym was in P.E. class in 19 . . . well, never mind what year it was. I got a B- in that class and a diploma that says I've completed the requirement. Done. Finito. Besides, when you exercise, your hair gets messy and you *sweat*, for goodness sakes. Oh, I mean per-spire. Nasty business. I prefer to avoid it all together.

"Yes, I know *she* likes to go to that new gym in town, but you have to admit, she is a little odd. I know she and a few of her friends seem to enjoy exercising, but you have to wonder about someone who prefers such pain and torture over chocolate. For the life of me, I cannot see the point. And why would anyone pay that kind of money to . . . have you *heard* what those dues cost? Imagine how many dinners at Bud and Lucy's Diner that would cover! Anyway, why would you want to pay money to go someplace to run around and get sweaty on purpose? I think it's a fad. If I wait it out long enough, it'll pass. . . . Oh, of course I know it's *good* for you. Where do you think I've been, Louise? Under a rock? 'Eat low-fat and exercise.' I know. I know. But it's too much like work. Besides, who has time? . . . Louise, get serious. You cannot mean you intend to join that woman at the gym. If you're tired and lethargic, the last thing you need to do is waste one ounce of your precious energy exercising. Sleeping Beauty didn't exercise. She napped. And she still got the prince. Now, darlin', come on over. I just made a chocolate turtle fudge cake. There's something that'll perk you right up!"

Come on. Admit it. Have you ever shared one of Mary-Margaret's complaints against exercise? It's time consum-ing. It can be painful. It's work. Yes, we know it's good for us, we know we should do it, but . . . and we fill in the blank with excuses or promises to do better. A stop at the gym or any other form of exercise is certainly not as popular in

119

many women's circles as say . . . chocolate turtle fudge cake. So I could just end this chapter right here with this:

Exercise. It's good for you. Just do it.

The end.

But Nike already said that. So let me counter Mary-Margaret's convincing argument with a few facts and this assertion: Lack of exercise and a sedentary, unfit body is a surefire ticket for Mama's trip south, while exercise and physical fitness is a powerful way to energize the body. I learned this from experience.

It was a time of great weakness in my life, only I didn't realize the extent of my weakness. It was my first dance with grief, and I stumbled through the steps as I thought everyone did, one awkward foot in front of the other. My mother, my mentor, my best friend, had died. I missed her terribly. I ached to pick up the phone for our Saturday morning chat that had been as regular as rain. One Saturday morning I even started for the phone before I remembered and stopped cold with a sick feeling in the pit of my stomach. I wanted to be able to tell her what new things the baby had done and ask her advice on . . . just about everything. No wonder I was depressed. No wonder I had no energy.

Daily life was full. I had four children ages nine and younger, a household to run, laundry I could never quite conquer, and a husband's needs to meet, however inadequately during that season. I accepted grief's accompanying depression in waves amidst the work. A good day here, a bad one there. I couldn't fall apart because, after all, I was a mom. People were depending on me. So I trudged through my duties and cried when I was alone, which either meant tub time or laundry time, and my washerwoman work brought some great tear time, because no child in their right mind *ever* goes near a woman doing laundry for fear of being recruited.

But one day was particularly bad. I struggled to get out of bed, and the bed won for several hours after I would have normally been up. I don't even remember what my preschoolers were doing. They were at a neighbor's perhaps, or maybe just watching *Sesame Street* in their pajamas. I plodded from the bed to the bath and just soaked in the tub for a long time. I finally decided to wash my hair and get dressed, but when I tried to open the shampoo bottle, I was so weak I couldn't manage to get it open. I tried again, dropped the bottle, and cried. Later, after I crawled back into my bed, I knew I needed some help, so I called a friend.

"I couldn't even open the shampoo," I cried.

"Lindsey, you need help," she said.

"I know. But not much help," I weakly protested.

"More than you realize."

"It's just a bad day," I justified. "I was fine last week, except for being constantly exhausted. I could make myself function properly if the kids were hurt or the house was on fire, but anything short of that just isn't worth the effort today because I'm so tired."

"I'm coming over, and you're going to the doctor," she said.

And I did. On the way there, I pictured myself filling out their paperwork. Reason for today's visit: *Inability to shampoo.* No, that didn't sound right. *Weakness in lid opening.* No. How about: *Hey, I'm just really sad and tired and exhausted and lethargic so just write a stupid prescription for someone to come do my laundry.* I knew what to expect. I would describe why I was there, the doctor would tell me I was suffering from depression, and I'd leave with an antidepressant. Simple. I wasn't thrilled about that, but if it would enable me to shampoo, I'd take it. Besides, I wasn't drooling or dropping food from my mouth or anything, so no white-coat escort was needed. Sitting in the doctor's office, I thought more about that laundry prescription.

She went through the spiel I expected, but then she talked to me about the whole-body importance of eating well and taking vitamin E, a bit unusual for most AMA trained physicians.

"Are you exercising at all?" she asked.

"Are you kidding?" I replied, looking at her like she'd asked me to sign up to be the first depressed woman in space. Doing the space shuttle laundry, no doubt. "No, I am not."

"You need to."

"Yes, everyone needs to, but you see, I have no energy. That's why I'm here. Now about that laundry prescription . . ."

"Seriously, you can take medication if you like, but you need to exercise. It will create more energy and combat depression."

On the way home, I stopped for the vitamins, decided to skip the antidepressants, then drove straight to a bookstore and bought books about women and stress and women and depression and . . . exercise. Maybe, just maybe, *reading* about exercise would do the trick.

"How in the world does that doctor expect you to exercise when you have no energy?" my aunt asked. I had no clue, but somehow, the next morning I dragged my exhausted body outside and managed to walk around the block. Slowly. *I hate this!* I thought. But I did the same thing the next day. The day after that, I walked around two blocks. And the next day. As I continued to make myself simply move my body, I gradually began to remember how good it felt when I used to run regularly.

I remembered being able to make my muscles work, how good it felt to work hard enough to sweat and breathe deeply, and how much energy I had after a workout. I continued my daily walks, gradually increasing my distance, time, and speed. And energy! I loved how I felt freshly showered after exercising, with energy for the first time in ages. I was amazed at the paradox that expending energy actually creates energy. I marveled at the incredible way God wired the mind and emotions to the body, that as I exercised I felt better physically and emotionally. My thoughts cleared. My depression lessened and then lifted. Energy and a lightness replaced the constant bone-aching weariness. I even shampooed my hair.

Research shows that exercise improves our mental outlook. At the University of Virginia, psychological tests were given to participants in that university's athletic program. A doctor described his analysis of those tests:

> We showed that there is some antidepressant effect with a sport that is not too vigorous, such as girls' softball. There is much more therapeutic value in something more active, like girls' basketball or tennis. But as for maximum results, jogging seems to offer the most sustained improvements. Jogging shows very measurable changes in depression levels before and after.[1]

When I was at an extremely low place, with muddled thinking, great sadness, and alarmingly little energy for daily life, exercise changed how I felt, thought, and functioned. It wasn't all I did, but the difference before and after I began exercising regularly was staggering. I am forever sold on the tonic of making physical activity and fitness a part of my life.

Benefits

God created our amazing bodies with a definite link between the spirit, body, and soul. Edward Greenwood, M.D., says this:

> The body and mind do not operate on different levels independently of each other. When one breaks down, the other suffers. Every change in the physiological state is accompanied by a change in the mental state; and every change in the mental state is accompanied by a change in the physiological state.[2]

By strengthening the body, we can improve the mind, and so on. If we want to be women who victoriously combat weariness in its varied forms, we can increase our capacity to do so through our physical bodies. Exercise increases our capacity to not grow weary!

This happens through the paradox of expending energy to create energy. One article said, "Thomas K. Cureton at the University of Illinois followed 2,500 adults through a physical conditioning program, and determined that the program helped people make friends, relieved tension, and increased their energy levels." Exercise also improves our sleep. When we lead physically active lives, we sleep better at night, and that's vital for fighting weariness. Just ask anyone who's battled insomnia! Exercise also increases our strength. A stronger body simply tolerates more weariness than a weaker one does. Exercise clears our thought processing as more oxygen reaches our brains. It releases endorphins that enhance our mood and fights PMS symptoms as well as anger and depression. It's amazing how a hefty dose of real throw-something-against-the-wall anger dissipates after a brisk walk around the block. Working out tones your muscles, which we know can help us avoid

124

the embarrassing situation of a child asking in public, "Mommy, why is the hang-down skin under your arms so jiggly?" (Tone those muscles, girls!) Being physically active acts like a giant Roto-Rooter, cleaning our internal pipes and preventing the plaque that silently builds up in our arteries when we enjoy a sedentary lifestyle. Exercise also oxygenates and helps purify our blood, ridding it of toxins that cause illness or disease and threaten to shorten our lives. Here's another perk: Nobel Prize–winning author/ researcher Albert Szent-Gyoergyi says that "physical exercise promotes syntropy—the tendency to reach higher levels of organization, harmony, and order."[3] What would we give, ladies, for a bottle of syntropy! And, of course, a lifestyle that includes regular exercise is vital to keeping our weight under control.

However, I want to get up on my soapbox for a minute about the weight control issue. One of the reasons so many women hate to exercise is because they see it from the limited weight-loss perspective. It becomes the loathed, or at least unfavorable, tool for shedding unwanted excess pounds (although I've never heard of *wanted* excess pounds). If we only think about exercise as that thing we have to do to lose weight, then no wonder we hate it. Let's replace the body sculpting, pain-and-drudgery image of exercise with the much more pleasant and healthy *fitness and health* mentality. Being thin may be our culture's goal (and our own, perhaps), but being physically fit should be the real goal. We want to be women with clean blood, healthy hearts, strong bodies. We want to be able to care for our families, do our jobs, and not grow weary in our well doing. At the very least, we want to be able to walk up a flight of stairs without sucking in air like Darth Vader.

When my girls became adolescents I wanted to instill in them a love for a physically active lifestyle and the benefits of regular physical exercise. I'd start discussing several things they could do to exercise.

"So, Mom, do you think I'm fat?" they'd ask.

"Certainly not!" I answered. And I began my quest to replace a culturally induced "exercise for weight loss" mentality with a "physical fitness means life and health" one. So they joined the swim team and had a blast. Now, years later, one daughter loves to walk and hike, and another is on the track team. Incidentally, they both look fabulous, and one lost twenty-five pounds over the past two years. But my greater joy is in the fact that in a culture that worships thinness and emphasizes exercise for weight loss, in a world where beautiful young women lose their perspective about their bodies and do dangerous things to be thin, my two sweeties share my enthusiasm for exercise as a means to the life-giving state of being physically active, healthy, and fit.

Exercise and Other Cultures

America glorifies working out, but not all cultures share our thinking. I recently read an article by an American who was on a lengthy stay in France. Her take on the matter was that she didn't see an exercising culture, and that many of the French thought our iron-pumping indulgence to be self-obsessed. Yet as a culture, the French tend to be thin in spite of a rather rich diet. As a wine critic, the American woman thought the answer lay somewhere between the red wine they drink and their lifestyle habits. The French tend to walk for transportation much more than Americans do. My daughter made the same observations when she visited China, Japan, and Thailand.

And think about those medieval folks. They didn't need to check their swords at Attila's Gym any more than the ancients living in biblical times contemplated working out. I am confident that Mary and Martha didn't sit around discussing their weight-lifting reps after they solved their I'm-working-harder-than-you-are tiff. Life itself was a workout and has been for millennia. It is only a fairly recent phenomenon that we must create "fake work" (exercise) to stay as healthy and active as our ancestors did. Yet honing and training the body wasn't completely foreign to our biblical ancestors, any more than it was to the Greeks before them who idolized the strong body and athletic prowess. Paul says in 1 Corinthians 9:27 that "I discipline my body and make it my slave," but his priority of the spiritual over the physical is clear in verse 25: "Everyone who competes in the games exercises self-control in all things. They then do it to receive a perishable wreath, but we an imperishable." Focusing on physical accomplishment, training, and the beauty of the human form needs to stay in perspective.

So How Much and What Should We Do?

Here's the super simple, needs-no-proven-research answer to what and how much, since we know it beats eating bonbons on the sofa: at least three sweats a week. And what to do? Anything you like that gets your heart rate up and keeps it up for at least twenty minutes. Do something that you enjoy and can look forward to, that feels more like fun than work. Choose something that's suitable to your temperament and season of life and is easy to stick with. Find something that can become a part of your lifestyle. I used to enjoy belonging to a health club. I loved the classes, the machines, the exercising companionship, and the post-workout whirlpool. But as my family grew, getting to the club with small children, a diaper bag, a snack bag, and a workout bag became more difficult. I was worked out by the time I'd arrived. As family and work demands increased, available time decreased, so I began to look for something to do that didn't include driving time. I then jogged for years, right up until my knees gave out and we moved to Colorado, where there is less oxygen in the air. Since I found it rather important to breathe while exercising, I discovered walking, which I've been doing for five years. (Well, actually, I've been walking for about four decades, but you know what I mean.)

For those searching for an exercise program that can be done easily and long-term, let me plug the virtues of walking. First of all, it's free, except for the cost of good walking shoes. It's easy to stick with, almost anyone can do it, it's as close as your front door, and many experts say the benefits rival those of jogging. It also makes a great companion to prayer. Morning walks are my daily dialogue with my Father. Occasionally I'll spend part of my return route listening to speaking tapes on a Walkman, but usually that time is an uninterrupted time to pray. When I received the book *PrayerWalk* by Janet Holm McHenry, I thought, *Sounds good, but I already know how to walk and pray. What's to learn?* Plenty. If you want to rev up your fitness and enhance your prayer life, read her book. Whether you walk, jog, take a class, play tennis, swim, or whatever, just make exercise a part of your lifestyle.

My friend Linda Vias has, in spite of being physically handicapped. The first day I saw her, she and her husband, Glen, were looking at the house behind ours with a realtor. I saw her cross the backyard on crutches and thought she had a broken leg. As we later became friends, I discovered her remarkable story. In her twenties she was a bright, healthy, long-distance runner and workaholic with a penchant for marathons and corporate ladder climbs. One day both ended when she fell chest-high into an uncovered manhole. The accident compressed a portion of her spine, which left her with no feeling in her legs and unable to walk. Yet Linda had no room for anger or questioning why it happened.

"Okay, this *did* happen," she said, "and it's not what I wanted. In fact, it stinks. But I'm on this journey with God, so even though there are a lot of mountains, through him we can conquer them. I'm not going to focus on the 'can't,' but on the 'can.'" Even though she used a wheelchair, she was unwilling to accept that she had to spend all day in it. She learned to "walk" with her upper body, swinging the dead weight of her legs through her "sticks," as she calls crutches.

Linda does more than many able-bodied folks do, more than the doctors ever thought possible, more than even she realized she could. She owns her own business, drives with hand controls, skis with special skis, plays wheelchair tennis, and does wheelchair racing. She swims, scuba dives, and snorkels, sails, bowls, and takes evening walks on her sticks with Glen and their children, Christian and Hope. When people comment that she looks too healthy to be in a wheelchair, she simply replies, "Well, I work out." She's even planning a hike near Pike's Peak with other disabled people for educational awareness in a world that often views those who are different as outcasts.

"I want people to know that I'm the same as you, it just takes me a *whole* lot longer to put on pantyhose! I'm in a wheelchair, but I'm excited about life, I am who God created me to be with the ability to still get out there and do things." Things some of us would never think possible. Like flying through the air on a trapeze. While visiting a circus school she and her daughter wanted to try the trapeze, but her son didn't, so she wanted to show him that he could.

A big Italian named Bruno carried Linda on his back up the tall ladder to the tiny platform.

"You're going with me, right, Bruno?"

"No, I carried you up the ladder. I pick you up and throw you, and you catch the bar."

She did!

Swinging back and forth high above the ground, she thought, *No wheelchair!* Total freedom. A little glimpse of heaven. When a spectator later commented on her daredevil attitude, she lovingly corrected her with the message she shares when she speaks to groups or to rehab patients struggling with their limitations. "This isn't about a show. I just enjoy what's offered. The world is only closed if we make it. Pushing limitations for the challenge isn't the point. Never say never. If you do, you limit yourself to not only yourself, but to what God can do in you."

If you think you're past your prime or limited in some way and there's no use in even trying, think again. Fanny Blankers-Koen was a sprinter from the Netherlands who won four events in the 1948 Olympics. She said, "A newspaper wrote that I was too old. It made me so mad that I went out and won four golds."

Exercise enhances our health, energy, performance, emotions, fitness, and sense of well-being. How we feel physically has great bearing on whether or not Mama's heading south, so for your sake and others', make fitness a personal growth goal.

Next, we'll look at the sleepy little topic of rest.

8

Road Weary

Recharging with Rest, Sun, and Air

"Come to Me, all who are weary and heavy-laden, and I will give you rest."

Matthew 11:28

Girlfriend, Get Some Rest

When I was little, my daddy liked to take family trips. I remember he'd get as excited as we did the night before a journey. We'd often leave early in the morning while it was still dark. He also liked to drink coffee from his green travel thermos while he drove, so that meant we got to take fairly frequent pit stops and occasional coffee-refill rest stops, with chocolate dip cones for us kids. While he and Mother refilled the thermos or ordered hamburgers or took the cooler with ham and cheese sandwiches out of the trunk, we'd stretch our legs and examine wild sunflowers growing along a fence and anything else we could explore. The rest stops were the best part of the trip.

Thankfully I married a man who likes leisurely paced travel as well. Once on a seventeen-hour trip we drove through a tiny Texas town and saw a hand-painted sign that said "Town Museum." Without hesitation we stopped to stretch and take in some unexpected sights. The change of pace and position was rejuvenating. But how often do we change the pace and position needed to rejuvenate our lives? Sometimes we live like some people travel, at full throttle without any rest stops. The destination may be reached faster, but at what cost?

Rest is such a pleasant word, isn't it? Funny how in a world with more time-saving conveniences than ever before in history, we suffer as a culture from a life lived in overdrive and filled with nonstop, exhausting activity. Rest is what we try to grab in between all the meaningful motion. One of the fastest ways for Mama to go south is to fail to get the rest she needs, that she was created to receive. Without adjusting our pace and rejuvenating body, mind, and spirit with rest, we will not be, cannot be, the women we long to be or the women we were created to be. We say and do things we shouldn't and fail to say and do things we should at times because we aren't rested. Angry mothers are often exhausted mothers. Unrested bodies create cloudy minds. Unrested spirits yield little fruit. When we fail to take vital rest stops, we go south and take others with us. And more alarming—when we are unrested, we are more open to spiritual attack, because the devil delights in our vulnerability. So remember this—*rest is a weapon!*

132

Kinds of Rest

Rest comes in various forms. Let me talk about four types: sleep, stillness, Sabbath, and soul rest.

Sleep

How much sleep do you average a night? Six hours? Seven? Some nights five? Chances are, not enough. We are a sleep-deprived nation, and most people don't really realize it. "Compared with 50 years ago, we sleep 2.5 fewer hours per night and work 10 more hours each week."[1] Many people routinely get less sleep than they need because they are used to what that feels like. Their lives are so busy that eight hours of sleep is considered a weekend-only luxury as they burn copious amounts of midnight oil to get everything done. Then they are jolted into each new day with an alarm clock. Periods of fatigue, sluggishness, or daytime sleepiness are seen as the norm, the cost of a full life, and they compensate with a cup of coffee or a Snickers bar.

This pattern may be culturally common, but it is not adequate rest, as studies prove.

> According to experts, getting just six hours of sleep a night is associated with increased daytime sleepiness, decreased performance, and a change in blood factors that promote the potentially dangerous process of inflammation. This can lead to a variety of problems, such as heart disease and hardening of the arteries, or atherosclerosis.[2]

Even this moderate amount of sleep deprivation causes "decreased vigilance and decreased ability to perform tasks that require coordination and thought."[3]

We've all heard that eight hours a night is optimal, but would you believe that some experts are saying we actually need nine hours a night? Why? Adequate sleep increases our brain function, rests our bodily systems, suspends the activity of our nervous systems, and helps our bodies rebuild and repair themselves when we sleep.

To improve the amount and quality of your sleep, try these tips. Try to go to bed at the same time every night and get up at the same time every morning, seven days a week. *Yeah, right. That's impossible,* you're probably thinking, and it is difficult, but when we do this, our bodies get into a pattern. Don't overeat or eat too close to bedtime. Sleep in a cool, well-ventilated room with adequate darkness. Don't consume caffeine or alcohol too late in the day. This can cause insomnia. For new mothers, take power naps daily when the baby sleeps and don't *ever* feel guilty about needing more sleep. Bearing, nursing, and caring for an infant is hard work from which we need to take a great deal of time and rest to rebuild our bodies. A family is much better served with a rested Mama, so if you must choose between vacuuming or napping, opt for the nap.

> When you lie down, you will not be afraid; when you lie down, your sleep will be sweet.
>
> Proverbs 3:24

Stillness

How often are you still? Do you have any "sit" time in your life when your purpose in sitting is not to eat, work, read, watch TV, or accomplish anything, but to purposely *stop* accomplishing? *Yeah, before I had kids,* you might think. "Before I became a working mother," others might say. Some people have temperaments that are so wired for activity and productivity that when confronted with the idea of just being still, they have the attention span of a three-year-old. But stillness is something we need in our lives beyond when we are sleeping. Stillness is a rare quality in today's world that has *nothing* to do with laziness or leisure or lack of motivation and *everything* to do with rest. Psalm 46:10 says, "Be still and know that I am God." Sure, we can pray and think about God as we're driving or doing a load of laundry, but God wastes no words. He instructs us to be still before him.

For years I didn't understand this idea of rest. Who had time for stillness? I was a busy mother with important work to do. Rest meant bedtime or crashing for a nap. I was only still during my Bible reading in the morning, but again, I was *doing* something. Gradually God has taught me the restorative power of stillness for body, mind, and soul. A. W. Tozer said that rest is not something we do; it is what comes to us when we cease to do. That is stillness. How much of it do you have in your life?

Our society is plagued with two things that fight with stillness: overscheduling and "hurrysickness" (a new word for a frantically paced lifestyle that was coined by sociologists). This frenetic pace trickles down into our children's lives, and many people are raising hurried, overscheduled kids. A researcher at the University of Minnesota wrote that in the past 20 years there has been a decline of 12 hours a week in children's free time, a 50 percent decline in unstructured outdoor activities, and a 33 percent decline in family dinners among families who have them regularly. Yet structured sports time has doubled.[4] In a well-intentioned effort to enrich our children's lives through multiple after-school activities, sports, lessons, and so on, we can end up tearing the fiber of family time and raising kids who lack stillness in their lives as much as we do. One thing that suffers is relationships. Tim Muehlhoff, in a *Discipleship Journal* article, agrees.

Unfortunately, relational depth is often a casualty in a hurry-sick world that glorifies exhaustion as a badge of accomplishment and accepts shallow relationships as the necessary price of achieving our individual ambitions. In contrast, Jesus states that those around us will know we are His followers not by our efficiency but by the quality of our love for each other (John 13:35).[5]

I've found the gift of stillness on a front porch. It's one of my most favorite things in life. My second favorite is a back porch. And a house with a side porch or (aaaah) a wraparound porch is sheer bliss. What more could a person possibly want? I'll tell you. Two or more rocking chairs and a porch swing to put on those porches, right next to the red geraniums and the chalkboard that cheerfully proclaims "Welcome!" That was my dream, which began when I was five years old and sitting out on our cement porch, waiting for hours for my grandma to arrive from Duncan, thirty miles away. A few years later I discovered *The Andy Griffith Show*. Andy would thank Aunt Bea for the fried chicken, grab his guitar, and head for the rocking chair on the porch. Sometimes he had important conversations with Opie or courted what's-her-name, but sometimes he just played his guitar or said stuff to Barney like, "Sure is hot," to which Barney articulated, "Yup," and Andy would say, "But it sure is a nice night," and Barney would reply, "Yup." The ice would clink in their tea glasses, the crickets would chirp, and my suburban-born-and-raised heart would be stirred with a vague longing for something as sweet and bewilderingly simple as porch sitting. Well, there was that brief "urban period" when I thought I wanted to live in a downtown loft with modern furniture and eat at bistros and listen to strains of jazz music mingled with city traffic. That's just the cup of tea for lots of folks, but eventually I meandered back to my southern roots and resumed wishing for a porch.

I've had a lifetime of longing for rural reality, and God has now answered the desire of my heart. Six months ago we moved "out to the country." I'm finally home, and I have found great contentment in my porch life and its rest. Our front porch is Southern style, covering the front of the house and (aaaah) wrapping around the side just a bit; the back porch looks out over a valley and the front range of the Rockies. I regularly sit in my white rocking chair next to my geraniums flanking the red front door and chalkboard sign proclaiming "Welcome!" and simply cease to do, even if just for a few moments. Amazing for an energetic, accomplishment-minded, formerly never-still woman with a large family.

My family often joins me for porch time. Last week my husband played John Denver and Eagles songs on the guitar while I just sat. The ice cubes clinked, the crickets chirped, the sun set. *Andy would be proud,* I thought. At the end of Tim's playing, the coyotes howled. "Thank you!" he replied and bowed to his audience. We moved from the back porch to the front to watch the moon rise, and soon all four kids joined us in the dark. We spent two hours that evening ceasing to do, wrapped in the simple joys of the love of family and the warmth of God's presence found so richly, so deeply in stillness. I was rested to the core of my being.

Whether it's two hours or ten minutes, on a porch or in a hotel lobby, during times of peace or snatched amid swirling chaos, everyone can find moments of rest in stillness. Remember our Father's words, "Be *still* and know that I am God."

Sabbath

The summer when I was ten, I read the Laura Ingalls Wilder Little House series. I'd ride my bike to the library, get the next book, and immerse myself in Laura's world. I wanted to be her that summer, except for how she spent her Sundays. She couldn't play or work or make noise. She spent time on a hard bench with her doll, trying to be a good girl on the Sabbath. *Sunday must have been torture,* I thought. No wonder our culture, even our church culture by large measure, has secularized Sunday. The blue laws of my girlhood that kept most retail stores closed on Sunday are gone, so we can shop all we want. We can work all we want. We can worship if we want. Laura's rule-focused, joyless, legalistic Sabbath and today's common, secularized Sabbath both miss the blessing that I believe God intended when he included Sabbath keeping in the Ten Commandments.

There is much to learn about the Jewish history, biblical implication, meaning, and application of the Sabbath, and it's fascinating, but in this small section, let me just offer a few ideas on this often ignored commandment that have been meaningful in my life and others'. The directive in Exodus 20:8–11 to remember the Sabbath day by keeping it holy, to work six days and make the seventh a Sabbath to the Lord our God, is a commandment for our blessing. It is God's prescription for our rest, offering restoration of our whole self. As John Anthony Page says in his article "The Gift of the Sabbath," "It is a day that is to be set apart—holy. It is a day in which we imitate our Creator by ceasing, as He did, from our creative labors."[6] It's more than a day off. It is a day to be purposeful about rest. To rest physically. To focus on God's presence and holiness. To cease doing what we normally do six days a week, just as God did.

Now there are many ways and interpretations of how to do this that are interesting to study, but we should avoid a legalistic set of how-tos, since Jesus tells us that "the Sabbath was made for man, and not man for the Sabbath" (Mark 2:27). It's a gift that we must first decide to accept, then continue to accept on a weekly basis. It's a time to change the pace of how we live the rest of the week, to get out of our work/accomplish/do mode. It's a holy day to focus on God and worship and the joy of living in him. It can also be a day for doing something restorative for your body, soul, and mind. That might mean taking a nap, playing volleyball, reading, hiking, or doing anything else that restores you for the coming week. If you work at a computer or do mental work all week, then physical activity can be as restorative as a nap. If your weekly work is largely physical, then rest your body. Whatever type of rest we need, let's protect our Sabbath day.

One Wednesday many years ago, I called my friend Brenda. "What are you doing today?" I asked my industrious, creative, disciplined friend. "Well, I had a great time of extended Bible study this morning, and I was just now lying on our trampoline, reading a book." In the middle of a Wednesday morning? I was surprised, since she normally would have been homeschooling or cooking or . . . busy at something. "We had a crazy, full day of church work and ministry all day Sunday. We worked as hard as any other day, so I'm taking my Sabbath today." Whether your Sabbath is observed from sunset Friday to sunset Saturday in Jewish fashion, on Sunday, on a regularly scheduled weekday as some pastoral families do, or even on an errant Wednesday if you missed your Sabbath that week, choosing to remember a Sabbath day is obedience in a world that has forgotten what that means. This is obedience that always brings joy and restoration. As we are told in Isaiah 58:13, we are to "call the sabbath a delight."

Soul Rest

This is my favorite kind of rest! It's a place of rest that we can find in the midst of any lifestyle or circumstance or place or activity level because of Christ within us. It is the rest that comes from the place of sweet surrender to him.

> "Come to Me, all who are weary and heavy-laden, and I will give you rest. Take My yoke upon you and learn from Me, for I am gentle and humble in heart, and you will find rest for your souls. For My yoke is easy and My burden is light."
>
> Matthew 11:29–30

Rest for my soul. Can there be anything more delightful? Right there in red letters Jesus promises us rest for our souls. I know about being weary. I'm a mom. I know about being heavy laden. I live in a world shaken by mass terrorism on our own soil, where mothers die and children get hurt, the good sometimes die young, and people we love reject God. A Mama who's headed south knows weary and heavy laden. It permeates her being like a yoke that not only weighs her down, but sometimes downright chokes her. That's why in the margin of my Bible next to this verse in Matthew, I circled "Come to Me" and wrote "like a hug from my Father!" Jesus gives me the sweet promise of soul-rest and calls my often weary and sometimes heavy-laden self to him like a daddy reaching for his baby.

Sometimes I get bogged down in the to-dos, the should-dos, the should-have-dones. At times my thoughts scream about the "injustice of it all," the "how will I do it all," and

140

the "you don't know what she said about me" or the "what do they think of me." Such thoughts weigh us down and are burdens that A. W. Tozer says are often rooted in pride and pretense from which "there is no release . . . apart from the meekness of Christ. . . . The rest He offers is the rest of meekness, the blessed relief that comes when we accept ourselves for what we are and cease to pretend."[7] What often wears us down is not what we do but how we think of ourselves and worry over what others think of us. Proverbs calls this the fear of man, and it is a snare.

In describing this use of the word *burden* in Matthew 11, Tozer says, "The word Jesus used means a load carried or toil borne to the point of exhaustion. Rest is simply release from that burden."[8] Work, mothering, and ministry can feel like heavy burdens and veer us down a southern road we don't want to travel. It's then we must remember to listen for our Father's voice whispering, "My child . . . come to me. My yoke is easy. My burden is light." Soul rest awaits us when we listen and come, bringing him our little offerings of love and service (like Sunday worship, book writing, grocery shopping, and toilet cleaning) and surrendering all we do and are to him. My prayer today as I write this is that I learn to enter his rest daily through the door of surrender, where peace and tranquility lie within, regardless of what swirls about me.

The Enemies and Benefits of Rest

Sleep, stillness, Sabbath, and soul rest have great enemies. Our culture, schedule, stress, fear, anxiety, chosen lifestyles, seasons of imbalance, workaholism, the "hurry-sickness" mentality so prevalent today, our focus on achieving and producing, sin, and attack from the enemy of God all work against us in our quest for rest. But women,

141

remember that we are designed to be receivers of all four types of rest. When we get enough sleep, add the beauty of stillness to our lives, take our weekly Sabbath, and enter into soul rest with our Father, we dramatically increase our capacity to grow and our ability to give joyfully. So go to bed earlier, sit on your porch, practice the Sabbath, and rest in his plan for your life.

Girl, Get Outside

Besides recharging our bodies with rest, we can recharge with two other surprisingly simple, free commodities: sunshine and fresh air. I went to high school in a brand-new building; we were the first class to use it and the first class to graduate from it. In spite of its beauty and newness, it had a major and not uncommon flaw—it was airtight, with windowless classrooms. Oh, the commons lunchroom had two-story windows, but where we spent the bulk of our day was hermetically sealed. From one view, the building could have passed for a prison. It felt like one too. This new building contrasted sharply with an older elementary school I had attended that had a wall of windows in the classroom, complete with bean plants growing on the sills, a view of grass, trees, and oleander bushes outside, and genuine operable windows that let in a breeze. The modern building was a prison, the other pleasant. The difference was simply sunshine and fresh air, two ingredients we need on a regular basis to stay healthy and alert.

Think how easy it is to insulate yourself in our adult world. Some people go from air-conditioned or heated houses through the garage to air-conditioned or heated cars and arrive at air-conditioned or heated offices and shopping malls, many with a short supply of windows and life-giving natural light. They return home, stopping by the mailbox in the car, and roll down the window just long enough to retrieve the mail. Then they hit the garage remote and return to insulated shelter, where they close the drapes, flick on the TV, and watch other people interact with the world.

If the climate is hot, humid, or snowy, this effect is magnified. I know several people who admit they hate to be outdoors; they prefer this kind of insulation. But it would make me insane. If we're not careful, we can live virtual lives, disconnected from bits of the earth around us that God made and we need. And this next generation of children is even more conditioned for the same thing, due to the plethora of electronics that keep them connected to everything but the great out-of-doors. As one mom told me, "My kids hardly ever play outside." This kind of insulated living is unhealthy for body and soul.

Fresh air is crucial to our health. Breathing a steady supply of stale, poorly circulated air breeds germs and makes us sick and promotes shallow breathing. "Sick building syndrome" is becoming increasingly common as people become ill from toxins in their buildings and even their homes. Building materials, carpets, furniture, and cleaning products give off invisible, odorless gases. Germs circulate through air ducts. Toxic mold grows. It's enough to make one want to pitch a tent outside.

Sunshine is also crucial to our health. When it shines on our skin, our bodies produce vitamin D and our calcium absorption is improved, which calms and enhances our immune and nervous systems. Getting natural sunlight is both relaxing and energizing, and sunlight is a great sleep enhancer. Ask any cat you know. But a walk outdoors in God's natural light can also wake us up. How can sunlight be both relaxing and energizing? It's "because all the natural ways of God are balancers. They balance out the body and make it whole."[9]

Natural light is linked to our mental health. Studies have proven the correlation between our mental state and the amount of light we receive. I've read that the suicide rate is higher in some cities that have a great amount of cloudy days and lower in cities that receive a great number of sunny days. Some people are deeply affected by seasonal light and experience varying degrees of depression during the darker winter days. Some cases of illness and depression are being successfully treated with light therapy. I don't need a study to tell me that, however. I cannot bear being in a dark environment—it makes me feel like a moth frantic to fly to the light. I lived for a time in a home that received little natural light. It was darkly paneled, had covered porches, and was surrounded by tall pine trees. It needed lamplight during the day, even in the summer. The house was also in a humid climate where we often went straight from heating to air conditioning, so the windows were rarely open. I occasionally had the blues in that house, and I know it was linked to the need for more light and fresh air.

The amount and type of light we receive also affects our productivity, brain function, growth, physical fitness, some health issues, and even life expectancy, some say. One study that examined the correlation between occupant productivity and daylight exposure in retail and school buildings showed that daylight and full-spectrum light exposure improved worker productivity, increased retail sales by 40 percent, and improved school test performance by 10 to 20 percent.[10] Another two-year study involving four kinds of light found that under full-spectrum light, students learned faster, tested higher, grew faster, had one-third fewer illness-related absences, and even two-thirds fewer cavities!

In short, we will live longer, healthier, more productive lives if we get regular light exposure. Natural sunlight is best, then full-spectrum lighting (which simulates the sun), then standard indoor lighting. Last on the list is fluorescent lighting, which we should avoid if possible. Take advantage of good weather days, and on days when the weather is too extreme, at least sit by the window for a bit. You don't have to live in Southern California to make the outdoors a part of your life. I've lived in a very hot climate where a person gets outside *very* early or not at all, and in very cold climates where a person learns how to layer. Add light exercise, like walking outdoors, and you have a deep-breathing, oxygen-enhancing, mood-lifting, lung-purifying, vitamin-D-making session in the air and sun that God provides for us. On really bad weather days or near the end of the winter season when I'm sick of the snow and move indoors to my treadmill, I greatly miss the benefits of sun and air on my face.

So, "Girl, get outside!" Find a way to add half an hour of air and sun to your life daily and see how much better you feel. Walk. Garden. Sit on the porch to read, work, or process the mail. I wrote a portion of this book on my porch. Grab the sun screen, shades, and a hat and avoid baking in the sun, but do expose yourself to God's wonderful tonic and elixir daily, even if just for fifteen minutes. The fresh air and healing properties of the sun are a quick, easy, free way to keep Mama from going south. We just need to remember to accept this gift from God.

Have you gotten enough sleep this week? Had any "down time"? Did you take a Sabbath day? Are you surrendering to God and the rest he promises for your soul regardless of what's simmering or storming in your life? Have you gotten outside to be rejuvenated with the healing properties of sun and light on your skin and fresh air in your lungs? Growing in these areas of your life can and will increase your capacity to serve others, and be healthier and happier while you're at it.

9

You Look Maaahvelous
Examining Beauty

The end of the morning dressing regimen: We stand at the mirror and smooth a stray hair into place, adjust our collar, and give our skirt a tug. There. Presentable. The TV-line-now-pop-culture-statement comes to mind: "You look maaahvelous." We turn for the profile view, which prompts us to instantly tighten our tummy muscles. On second thought, we decide we look . . . okay. Maybe.

Beauty. We admire it. Long for it. Strive for it. Spend money, time, and attention on it. We carefully examine ourselves to see if we've achieved it in the morning. But what is beauty, really? Is it important to our personal growth? To answer that, I'll ask another question.

What do you look like? I don't mean just the color of your hair and eyes. What do people see when they look at you? What does it matter, anyway? It's all superficial, vain, and unspiritual, right? Well, it often is, but let me offer another perspective.

To some, beauty evokes positive images of artfully applied makeup, stylish clothing, a perfect haircut, and (sigh) new shoes. (My daughter Allison has swooned over new shoes since she was five and has been able to spot a shoe department six aisles out.) Others grimace in disgust at the topic of beauty, thinking of their imperfect features and extra poundage or seeing it as a frivolous time waster, obviously unimportant to God. Which view is correct? To answer that, instead of examining ourselves, let's examine beauty in three categories: our bodies' appearance, maintenance, and countenance. The Bible says our bodies are God's temple, so appearance is window dressing on the temple (looking sharp), maintenance is the routine care of the temple (good grooming), and countenance is the outward expression of our inner man (facial expression). When others see us, they see a reflection of all three.

Appearance

Why Does It Matter?

Our appearance matters because our bodies are the temple of the Lord. For those of us who do not live alone, it matters because our families see us each day. We want to be pleasing to our husband, and by God's design, they notice how we look. Our children notice too. One of my teenage daughters told me recently, "Mom, thanks for not looking, well, old and nerdy." A high compliment.

Next our appearance matters because we live in community with others. In community, we are obviously with people. Others see us. Profound, I know, but think about it. What do they see? What does that outward view say of the inward person? Do we appear to be women with the abundant life of which Scripture speaks? Are we attractive? (Not just in the physical sense, but the whole ball of wax.) Do others see us and want what we've got, or do they see "dowdy" written about us and prefer to steer clear?

Speaking of steering, here's a little story. When my older daughters were in elementary school, I had a little dilemma one day that tested this theory of appearances, especially of first impressions. I went to my car to go pick up my daughters, but the battery was dead. Dead again, should I say. (Can't anyone make an automatic shut-off interior car light?) I called my neighbor to borrow her car. Sure, she said, until she discovered her car wouldn't start either. In a moment she called me back and said, "Hey, my friend is here, and she said you can use her car. It works, by the way." Relieved, I walked to her house and scooted off in the borrowed car to get my children.

I was breathing a prayer of thanks for this woman's generosity and working battery when I pulled into the car pool line. The children on the sidewalk nearest me began to snicker. A few kids farther down the line began to point at my car. Next to them were my girls, who smiled along with their friends. I heard Jacquelyn say, "Boy, I feel sorry for whoever's getting picked up in that car!" Then they recognized that their own mother was driving the object of this minor commotion and that they were the unfortunate riders. I inched forward in this loud, lime green, dilapidated . . . well, there's no other word for it . . . low rider. I even vaguely remember fuzzy dice. The car stood out against the other mothers' minivans like a seventies disco dancer in a church full of Baptists. My girls were horrified. And to add insult to injury, I'd never "fixed up"

149

that morning. No shower. No makeup. Just poorly dressed "raw beauty" on a bad hair day. The girls slunk into the car and practically slid to the floor to escape view. I thought it funny that their entire class was laughing.

"Mother, how could you!" they said. "But girls, we're having an adventure!" They rolled their eyes. "Really," I insisted. "And it's even an answer to prayer." They shut their eyes and slumped lower. Undaunted, I drove to the kindergarten to pick up my son. My daughters got to be seen by even more people they knew from our neighborhood as I roared into that school in the low rider, laughing so hard I could barely drive. My son, smart little boy, was thrilled! "We'll never get over this, Mom," my daughters wailed. "All these people think we are *so* weird. No one will believe we're normal." They needed no lesson in the power of first impressions based on appearance, and they went on to discuss changing schools or moving out of state. However, I'm happy to report that they are now teenagers and only occasionally need therapy for the event.

Whether we like it or not, we make an impression on others. People draw conclusions about us based on what they see. "So what? I don't care what others think about me," you may say. But that brings us to the next reason our appearance matters.

It affects our *influence*. While we will never please everyone, nor should we try, we mustn't be naive. What others see can affect what they hear. In other words, our appearance can help or hinder other people's ability to hear our hearts, and that is important. A beachfront evangelist will better connect with those he wants to minister to in cut-offs than in a suit and tie. My husband relates well to his colleagues and shares his faith in his corporate world as a professional, which includes how he dresses.

One may say, "I'm me, regardless. I won't dress to please people." That's fine, but I'm not talking about pleasing people, I'm talking about influencing them. We don't need to be popular. We do need to realize that our appearance can be an asset or a stumbling block to what we want to communicate to others. Here are two contrasting illustrations of that point.

My friend Brad, a newly growing Christian, had been influenced and challenged in his faith by Roger, a friend of his. One day Roger invited him to meet a group of his friends over coffee. Brad enjoyed the thought-provoking conversations he and Roger shared, so he looked forward to the meeting. However, Brad was taken aback when he met Roger's group. "The girls startled me," he said. "They had these severe, horrible hairstyles and weren't wearing any makeup. They looked like they had picked the ugliest shoes and dresses they could find at the Salvation Army. People in the Starbucks were literally staring at us. All I could think of was to end the evening as quickly as possible. I didn't want to be guilty by association."

They were sweet girls and had something worthwhile to say, but my friend could not hear them. He couldn't get past their appearances to hear their hearts.

Conversely, another friend of mine, speaker and author Carol Kent, always looks like a million bucks. She's the epitome of a polished professional woman who knows how to make her makeup, wardrobe, and accessories sing, ever so tastefully. She once shared this story with me. She had arrived at a speaking engagement eager to share her message with what she'd been told was the sweetest group of ladies. She wasn't told, however, that their denomination did not believe in wearing makeup or jewelry. There she sat on the front row, waiting for them to introduce her, wearing a brightly colored suit, bright lipstick, and perfectly coordinated jewelry. During the prayer she quietly removed her earrings and necklace and tucked them in her purse. She took off her bracelet and extra ring. Then she took a tissue from her bag and wiped off her lipstick. Why? For their approval? Because she wants to be liked everywhere she goes? Hardly.

"I did that because I didn't want my appearance to stop them from hearing what I had to say," she said. "I wanted to be respectful to them, and more important, I wanted them to hear my heart." Right or wrong, our appearance impacts our influence.

Another reason our appearance matters is that it affects how we feel and perform. I currently home-school my children and require them to come to the table dressed for the day of lessons. Past experience has shown that routinely sloppy dress produces sloppy work habits. And I for one feel better and more productive when I start my day cleaned up. I remember going on a field trip to the Houston Symphony with my children years ago, and one of the moms organizing the outing suggested we have our children dress up. "If they dress like they're going to the park," she said, "they tend to behave like they're at the park. If they dress for the symphony, they behave more like little ladies and gentlemen." Exceptions noted, but that experience has stuck with me through the years.

Another reason our appearance matters is that God has a thing or two to say about beauty. Right now I'm looking out my study window at the most beautiful orange sunset slipping beneath the purple-hued mountains and newly budding green trees. If beauty were something to be avoided to attain greater spirituality, then our Creator would have to remake most of his creation.

Approaches

So what is beauty in a woman? A great deal more than our culture portrays, but for the sake of this discussion on physical appearance, one thing we could all agree on is that it is quite subjective. Is Barbara Streisand beautiful or plain? Which is more pleasing to the eye—blond or brunette, tall or short, olive complexion or peaches and cream? Tailored clothing or flowing romantic fabrics? Jeans and boots or skirts and pumps? Big jewelry or no jewelry? Glamour-girl coverage or no makeup at all?

Physical beauty and its window dressing are truly in the eye of the beholder, accounting for different tastes, style preferences, worldviews, and cultural influences. Beauty is defined and expressed in various ways, from pop culture (Britney Spears), to cross-culture (African women), to counterculture (spiked hair to head coverings). If you really want to open a can of worms, ask a group of Christian women from diverse backgrounds what should be worn in church.

One woman I know is very flamboyant and believes if accessories are worth anything, then one should be able to be seen from across the room. She owns bright scarves, hair jewelry, and feathers. Another woman I know believes in being completely unadorned. No jewelry, no makeup, and she owns a snood, a crocheted head covering worn in public.

So what should or shouldn't we think about beauty? Let me suggest a few wrong attitudes and some right ones on the topic from a biblical perspective.

Wrong Attitudes

1. Vanity

Vanity can be easy to spot with its "I look maaahvelous" attitude, which is quite ugly. When I was eight years old,

153

a friend's mother came to pick me up to play at her house. She didn't come in or even come to the door when she arrived. I vividly remember her preoccupation with applying bright-red lipstick. I noticed her lips looked plenty red to begin with. When I got in the car, she tossed me a hi and tweaked her heavy makeup some more. She never even looked at me. Only at her image in the rearview mirror. I later learned that some of my mother's friends didn't much care for the woman. The word they used was *vain*. But I already knew what that meant. It meant someone who likes lipstick better than she likes an eight-year-old girl.

Scripture says not to think more highly of yourself than you ought and that beauty is vain. Further, it says, "If you have been foolish in exalting yourself . . . put your hand on your mouth" (Prov. 30:32) and that haughty eyes are one of the seven things God hates. This would explain why he hates vanity as defined as "inflated pride in oneself or one's appearance." Pride is simply sin—something we all experience. It's easy to think back on my friend's mom as a depiction of vanity, but the line between grooming and vanity blurs a bit as it edges into my adult world with a soft focus. How often do I cross that line? How often do you? We can creep over the line of vain, self-inflated thoughts in full view of a crowd or in the middle of ministry, and skip right back again undetected, because it's a silent sin of the heart. My prayer is for God to take captive my thoughts when they wander into this dangerous playground and to remind me of one of my life verses: "God forbid that I should glory save for the cross of our Lord Jesus Christ" (Gal. 6:14 KJV).

2. INSECURITY

This is vanity's other side. Instead of "I look maaah-velous" thinking, it's more like this: "My stomach has more rolls than Parker House, my cellulite thickens hourly, my wardrobe stinks, and I'm having a bad hair year. Culture is right. I'm disfigured." Our grocery list of imperfections stays close to our hearts, in our front pockets, threatening to jump out and ruin perfectly good moments. When we're out with a friend, the list screams at us, "Have you forgotten about me? Quit enjoying the moment. Your hair is frizzy, and hers isn't." In the middle of worship, it sings, "How could you possibly have worn this today?" While making love to our husband, it whispers, "He doesn't really think you're beautiful. He's just enduring you." And those thoughts, my friends, are destructive. We can be so filled with insecurity over how we look that we don't even see this for what it really is . . . vanity's sister, taking up far more of our thought lives than what pleases the Father.

A contrasting picture is seen in the Song of Solomon, in which the bridegroom lavishes his praise on his beloved and her appearance. "How beautiful you are, my darling. How beautiful you are," he says. She doesn't think, *Yeah, but wait till we're in the tent tonight, fella. You have no idea what you're really getting. I have this little list . . .* No, indeed. She says, "I am black but lovely." And she has nothing to hide. "Why should I be like one who veils herself beside the flocks of your companions?" When was the last time you thought, *I'm lovely to my husband. I'm lovely to my God*?

3. IDOLATRY

This is the next stepping stone of wrong attitudes that flows from vanity or insecurity. We become so absorbed with how we look, either good or bad, that our appearance becomes an idol in our lives, controlling how we behave, taking precedence God never intended. Take Lauren for instance. She would rather have her teeth drilled than be seen without makeup. The last time she allowed this to happen was at the kidnap breakfast in college. She's worn makeup to bed ever since. And Tina has a disciplined beauty regimen that she never misses. It takes two hours a day, every day. Lauren and Tina may be in danger of letting their physical appearance become their idol.

Attention to our appearance can become idolatry when we attach significance to it that God never intended, like when we equate it with love and acceptance. One of my friends recently confided that she'd really been convicted in this area. She'd spent most of her adult life terribly insecure about her list of imperfections and dissatisfied with all her "disfigurements." She was petrified at the thought of getting married and was convinced that no one could ever love her. When she met someone who did, she was on cloud nine. Such unconditional love illuminated her need to analyze her thinking patterns about appearance. She'd sacrificed acceptance in her life on the altar of looks. Realizing that—calling it for the biblical term that it is, idolatry—and repenting of it has been a paradigm shift for my beautiful friend. "It's been painful to realize the importance I've placed on how I look or don't look and to see how I've tied that to other areas of my life. Conviction of this sin hurts, but God is freeing me and changing how I think." As Paul says, "Little children, guard yourselves from idols" (1 John 5:21).

4. NEGLECT

Another wrong attitude about our appearance is neglect, the habitual disregard for how we look. If we are to present our bodies as living sacrifices as Scripture says, that does not mean we should neglect them. There is nothing more spiritual about disheveled, greasy hair and dirty, unkempt clothing. Perhaps some, in their attempt to "be ye separate" have even thought their nonattentiveness to appearance is somehow holier, but Jesus addressed this attitude in Matthew 6:16–17.

> "Whenever you fast, do not put on a gloomy face as the hypocrites do, for they neglect their appearance so that they will be noticed by men when they are fasting. Truly I say to you, they have their reward in full. But you, when you fast, anoint your head and wash your face . . ."

Whether we're fasting or not, neglecting our appearance has nothing to do with holiness.

A few women even reject beauty entirely, focusing on the "beauty is vain" verse and missing the fact that Scripture does not prohibit adornment. While we see in 1 Peter 3:4 that our emphasis is clearly to be "the hidden person of the heart," neglecting our appearance has nothing to do with attaining the gentle and quiet spirit God desires.

5. Anxiousness

The last wrong attitude I'll mention is anxiousness about our wardrobes. This can be a challenge when we have an event that needs attire we don't own, and we have one hour at a crowded mall to find something appropriate. Or if pregnancy suddenly makes the wardrobe obsolete and there's not enough money to visit Pea in the Pod or anywhere else. We feel justified in experiencing wardrobe stress, but Scripture calls this being anxious and says we shouldn't. "And why are you anxious about clothing?" (But God, have you seen my closet?)

> "Observe how the lilies of the field grow; they do not toil nor do they spin, yet I say to you that not even Solomon in all his glory clothed himself like one of these. But if God so clothes the grass of the field, which is alive today and tomorrow is thrown into the furnace, will He not much

more clothe you? You of little faith! Do not worry then, saying . . . 'What will we wear for clothing?' . . . for your heavenly Father knows that you need all these things."

Matthew 6:28–31

He has seen our closets after all. So I don't think he minds if I pray before shopping.

Now let's move from wrong attitudes about our appearance to some right ones.

Right Attitudes about Beauty

1. *We are the temple.* "Do you not know that you are a temple of God and that the Spirit of God dwells in you . . . for the temple of God is holy, and that is what you are" (1 Cor. 3:16–17). The fact that my body houses God's Spirit is phenomenal. We should honor God with our bodies, but nowhere in Scripture does God tell us how our temples are to appear, except to give a dire warning for anyone who destroys this body temple. So there is great latitude for our common sense and cultural and historical differences. When I was studying Old Testament history with my children this year, we read about the temple that David planned and his son Solomon built. It was magnificent, and I was struck by the great attention to the beauty of the structure, all to honor God because he resided there. Then I noticed that God approved and sanctioned the temple's beauty. Nowhere do we read that he said, "You, Israelites. Make it ugly so I'll know your hearts are pure." The temple was a feast for the eyes, and it glorified God.

2. *We are to please our husband.* A quick look at beauty in the Bible takes you past a parade of women who were called beautiful—Sarah, Rebekah, Rachel, Job's daughters, Abigail (who was called intelligent *and* beautiful), Bath-

sheba, and Esther, to name a few. I noticed that their beauty was linked to their husbands. The Bible does not say that they were beautiful and became movers and shakers in the town. Psalm 45:11 says of a bride, "Then the King will desire your beauty." True for brides then, true for brides today, and this reference to Israel. God has wired men to be attracted by our physical appearance, so we need to remember that our beauty is for the pleasure of our husband. No one else. Growing as a woman in beauty is a gift to our mate.

3. *We are ambassadors.* "Therefore, we are ambassadors for Christ, as though God were making an appeal through us" (2 Cor. 5:20). An ambassador represents a king, in our case the King of kings. If we were suddenly appointed ambassador to France, would we arrive at our post looking like we were headed for a volleyball game? No, we'd look the part and honor our president. There's no political protocol that goes with our job descriptions as ambassadors for Christ, but it doesn't hurt to ask, "Do I represent the King well today?"

4. *We are God's creation.* Everything God made during the six days of creation was beautiful. Sunrises and sunsets. Ocean and lakes. A mountain meadow. Step outside on a clear summer night and marvel at the stars. Visit the zoo and be amazed at the beauty of powerful animals and iridescent birds. We too are one of his beautiful creations, made in his image. Like Michelangelo knew, the human form is beautiful.

5. *It's temporal.* Our physical beauty is short-lived. Man's physical days are but a vapor that withers and fades like the grass. Beauty is temporary, but godliness is eternal.

6. *God looks past our appearance, good or bad.* "For God sees not as man sees, for man looks at the outward appearance, but the Lord looks at the heart" (1 Sam. 16:7).

159

This is the beginning of real beauty; beauty that matters because it is what matters more to God. In a world fixated on everything young, thin, and as near to perfect as photography can create, we would do well as women to remember this verse. It's a tonic for insecurity and vanity, good hair days and bad, natural beauty and disfigurement. A lovely appearance and an ugly heart make an ugly woman.

7. *It's not of great value.* The Proverbs 31 woman was a sharp dresser. We are told she wore purple linen—a fine fabric and a royal color (purple dye was not common). So while Scripture mentions that she cared about how she dressed and did it well, it's all put into perspective in the last verse. "Charm is deceitful and beauty is vain, but a woman who fears the LORD, she shall be praised" (Prov. 31:30).

Growing in Beauty

We can honor God with our temples, please our husbands, represent the King well, and accept that our forms are beautiful, but we must always balance those attitudes with the truth that our beauty is temporal and of little concern to God compared to our hearts.

So what should we pursue to grow as beautiful women?

A beautiful heart. "Your adornment must not be merely external—braiding the hair, and wearing gold jewelry, or putting on dresses; but let it be the hidden person of the heart" (1 Peter 3:3–4). We have Old and New Testament references to appearance with the emphasis on the heart. What's in yours?

A gentle and quiet spirit. These are the components of a beautiful heart. 1 Peter 3:4 says, "But let it be the hidden person of the heart, with the imperishable quality of a gentle and quiet spirit, which is precious in the sight of

God." How difficult that can be at times! But how worth it. When we attain it, it's imperishable—it won't decay (like beauty). A gentle and quiet spirit is indestructible! I love that God wrote this specifically to you and me as women. How sweet of the Father to tell us what is precious about us to him.

Submissiveness. What? you may silently shriek. *What's that word doing in a chapter about beauty?* It seems submission was a beauty essential of our spiritual predecessors. "For in this way in former times the holy women also, who hoped in God, used to adorn themselves, being submissive to their own husbands" (1 Peter 3:5). In spite of intelligence, good ideas, strength, common sense, intuition, independence, and a host of other traits that we use to counter submission, submitting to our husbands with a gentle and quiet spirit is the most beautiful adornment we women can wear.

Modesty. We are a culture that has lost its modesty. Just watch TV for five minutes, look at a billboard while driving, watch the Academy Awards, or attend a public gathering and look around. Immodesty abounds. Our culture reeks with the gross display of inappropriate, sensual, provocative attire in the name of freedom and self-expression. It must grieve God's heart for women to share with the world what he meant for them to share with their husbands only.

Recently a friend married a man who was of a stricter denomination than she was. She was always modest and tasteful in her dress, but the church's standards were a challenge for her at first. She looked at how some of the other women there dressed, and she thought, *I want to please the Lord and my husband, but I cannot do ugly.* As her dear friend, I was glad to hear that. But she decided the issue was not just interpretation of Scripture and its application, but also modesty and what that meant to her husband, so she asked for *his* definition. "To me, this means please don't show your cleavage," he said, "or your thighs, or the form of your breasts." And those were concrete guidelines she could live by. Nothing low cut. No short shorts. No tight tops. Within his parameters she was free to dress as beautifully as she wished in public, and, as he hoped, as provocatively as she wished for him alone.

Definitions of modesty will vary among individuals, but I think we need to back up a few steps from our culture's definition and regain lost ground. Modest dressing needn't be Victorian, yet should we condone our Christian teenage girls dressing like Britney Spears?

The author of *Beautiful Girlhood,* a book written for young girls a long time ago, says,

> But it remains a fact that many nice women dress in a way that is not strictly modest. Many do not think, they just do as the rest do. It is the same with some women who profess to love the Lord. Their minds and hearts are not awake on this line. They follow where the present fads lead with no thought of the consequences.[1]

If women go south in their appearance through less-than-modest dressing, they can take young girls with them through the example they set. The author goes on to give good advice, for young girls as well as us: "We must have a conscience toward God ourselves, and answer these questions before Him in our own hearts. As for myself I cannot wear what I know is not becomingly modest for a Christian to wear."[2]

Femininity. As a culture we've not only lost our modesty, we've lost our great distinction of valuing femininity and reflecting it the way women of the past did. I love histori-

162

cal movies, especially the English ones, for the clothes more than anything else. I imagine wearing sweeping skirts and upswept hair (although corsets never enter my daydream). There is just no mistaking the beauty of femininity.

I recently had a conversation with one of my daughters about this. She was quite surprised to hear that the 1960s were the watershed years of pants, that Jackie Kennedy Onassis and Katherine Hepburn were trendsetters for publicly donning dungarees, and that both of her grandmothers had worn hats and gloves. We sipped tea cross-legged on the floor in our jeans and talked about how we both felt really nice when we wore dresses. "We ought to wear them more often!" we said. My older daughter joined us and confirmed our point by looking lovely in her skirt. Comfortable cotton dresses and swingy skirts with sandals in the summer, long, warm skirts and boots in the winter, we decided. It felt, well, so feminine. However, we live in the country, and my nine-year-old daughter needs more convincing. She loves to play in the dirt, jump on the trampoline, and ride her bike in her jeans. (I love to play in the dirt too, although I call it gardening.) We're all keeping our khakis and Levis, but her sisters and I are touting the value of our feminine things at every turn.

A nonjudgmental heart. This is a beautiful thing to pursue. Women can sometimes be catty, proffering opinions where they aren't needed. We need to give one another grace and let our personal convictions and style preferences be our own standards, and not force them on our sisters. "Therefore let us not judge one another anymore, but rather determine this—not to put an obstacle or a stumbling block in a brother's way" (Rom. 14:13).

A Few Tips

When I first envisioned this chapter, I thought I'd gather some great beauty tips or have a makeover done in the name of research. But ultimately I didn't want to write about the merits of waxing versus shaving. So here are a few tips from a woman who depends on her friend's fashion advice, like this little gem she once offered me: "If you show up in 'suntan' pantyhose, I'll smack you." I learned the new color was "oatmeal."

- No matter what you wear, let it *be clean, neat, and pressed.*
- *Be yourself.* I've read several books and have received good advice in the past about how to dress when speaking publicly. I hate to shop, so choosing appropriate clothing for speaking was one part of my ministry I disliked. Once I spoke at a women's conference, after the agony of securing an appropriate garment. The outfit met all the "rules"—it was professional, modest, an appropriate shade of lilac for spring, and had matching shoes. Yet when I got there I felt like a cross between an Easter egg and the Church Lady. That night after the conference, I changed into my regular clothes—sandals with heels, a comfy long black skirt, top, an open jacket with the sleeves pushed up, and silver jewelry. Several of us gathered in the room of Kathy Troccoli, who had been the musical artist for the conference. "Girl, *that's* what you should have worn today!" she said. I fell on her bed, bewailing my wardrobe dilemma, and she explained that she'd been surprised at my "style shift" from when we first met. She helped me see I'd been so busy following the rules, I was not being myself. Since then, I've ditched

164

the Easter egg suit, dressed appropriately (but also like myself), and have often left the podium to sit on a stool and share my heart without once feeling like the Church Lady. Being myself frees me to focus on other people.

- *Dress appropriately for the situation.* Going from a professional environment to a soup kitchen calls for a change of clothing. I once heard an excellent speaker telling of her adventures ministering in a Mexican jungle, but when she said, "I was running down this hillside in my little Laura Ashley jumper . . ." I thought, *A Laura Ashley outfit in the jungle?* I should have ignored her comment, but I missed her whole point as I imagined the juxtaposition of her, her setting, and those to whom she was ministering.

- *Don't be afraid of change.* We really do not want to look like we did in high school. Whether your style is classic or trendy, stay balanced and tasteful. Sometimes when shopping I remind myself, "You are not Jennifer Aniston."

Appearance is just one aspect of beauty—the window dressing. Let's look at our bodies' maintenance next—the routine care of our temples.

Maintenance

The performance and looks of a car depend on how well and regularly it is maintained. As do our bodies. Good grooming is the backbone of beauty, much the way cleaning and decluttering is the backbone of home decorating. Good grooming is the essential that is available to us all regardless of income and position, regardless of how much natural beauty we have or don't have, and regardless of what we have at our disposal to enhance our appearance. It's simple, it can be inexpensive, and it takes just a few moments a day.

In our society good grooming tends to be the norm, with daily hair washing, blow-dryers, nail salons, and the like. Of course, being a new mom, having a large family, or being ill or highly stressed can take its toll on our grooming routines. An older woman once mentioned to me a scheduling dilemma since "weekly nail appointments might get in the way." I remember thinking, *Yeah, right. I have four kids eight and under including a newborn, a husband who travels, and a tight budget.* There are seasons for extreme simplicity.

Here are a few favorite grooming essentials: Maintain clothing (no holes, stains, or runs), that favorite nappy sweatshirt excluded. Consider sunscreen on face and hands as essential as underwear. It's cheap insurance against skin cancer and wrinkles, both of which are to be avoided at all costs. Choose a haircut that's good for your facial shape and fits with your lifestyle in regard to styling time. Pay attention to your hands and nails. I was once sized up by someone based on the condition of my hair and nails (which happened to be good that day). And I still remember a girl in high school who thought one coat of red nail polish was good for months. She always looked a bit dirty. And speaking of dirt, remove it and cosmetics from your face every night. Someone once said that sleeping in your makeup one night ages your face three days. Since no one can actually *prove* this, I say bank on it just in case! Use lotions, creams, and oils with gentle upward strokes (remember ladies, we are not kneading bread here). In fact, slather it on while you're at it. What can it hurt in the fight against alligator skin and wrinkles?

To make sure you are maintaining your temple, try this: (1) Assess your thinking about it. Regular good grooming

166

is not selfish or unspiritual, but don't go off the deep end overindulging time and money on it. (2) Assess your maintenance habits. Is there anything that you could improve? (3) Make it a part of your routine.

Now to the final and perhaps most important aspect of beauty—our countenance.

Countenance

"A joyful heart makes a cheerful face, but when the heart is sad, the spirit is broken" (Prov. 15:13). As this verse says, what's in our hearts we wear on our faces. Have you ever seen someone dressed to the hilt, perfectly maintained, coiffed, and manicured, but with a face full of anger? What stood out more, their appearance or their facial expression? Probably their expression. The biblical word for this is our *countenance,* and it is a reflection of our hearts and emotions. It is the outward expression of the inner man. So what use is it if we work on our maintenance and appearance and then spoil everything by forgetting about the importance of our countenance?

What do people see when they look at our faces? We tend to check our appearance and maintenance in the morning. We look in the mirror, see that we are presentable, and walk away remembering what we look like. But not so with our countenance. Have you ever seen your reflection in a mirror during a moment of anger? I happened upon mine once accidentally, and it scared me to death. *Oh, how horrid I look,* I thought. Anger is just one thing that affects our faces. In *The Heart of Anger,* Lou Priolo lists eight attitudes of the heart that can mar the countenance. They are pride (Ps. 10:4), anger (Gen. 4:5), bitterness (Gen. 31:1–2), fear (Dan. 5:5), sensuality (Prov. 6:25), rebellion (Prov. 30:17), guilt (Ezra 9:6–7), and selfishness (Prov. 23:6).[3] Scripture even mentions how talking badly about others affects our faces. "The north wind brings forth rain, and a backbiting tongue, an angry countenance" (Prov. 25:23).

I want to contrast that with two positive things Scripture says about our countenance. "A man's wisdom makes his face to shine and the harshness of his countenance to be changed" (Eccles. 8:1). How I pray for a heart of wisdom! After Moses encountered God on Mount Sinai, he came down with his face radically altered, glowing because he had seen the Lord. In heaven we will experience a face-to-face relationship with God, like Moses did, but we are told that even now in this life, God's face can change us. "The LORD lift up His countenance on you, and give you peace" (Num. 6:26). And this: "How blessed are the people who know the joyful sound! O LORD, they walk in the light of Your countenance" (Ps. 89:15). God's face, his presence, is a source of peace, light, blessing, and joy. Since I know that "in His presence is fullness of joy" and that "He inhabits the praise of His people," I know that praise is the place to alter my face. I want to grimace and wear fatigue, stress, and anger *less*. I want to smile more.

No matter what we see when we look in the mirror, God sees us as lovely and is "enthralled with our beauty" (Ps. 45:11). Nancy Stafford, a former Miss Florida and the author of *Beauty by the Book,* agrees: "Real beauty isn't what we see in magazines or on movie screens, and it doesn't depend on the opinions of others or the changing tastes of culture. True beauty is seeing ourselves as God sees us, reflected in the mirror of His word."[4]

As I grow, I pray that my face reflects the fact that I am a receiver of so much from God, that his countenance shines on me, and that I replace countenance-marring attitudes with godly fruit that is seen when people see me. Let us all strive to be women whose appearance, maintenance, and countenance are beautiful because we have a heart that seeks God's.

Part 3

Side Trips South, Deep Within
The Soul

10

Oatmeal or Rocket Science
Expanding Our Minds

Have you thought recently about where you are in the gray-matter continuum? This can be quite frightening. From "pregnancy brain" to senior moments, we sometimes find ourselves facing an open refrigerator when it dawns on us that we're looking for our keys. Or maybe we're trying to instruct our children to pick up something off the floor, and we sense our brain eking along like a train on rusty tracks as we sputter, "And pick up those . . . those . . . [eek, grind, processing now] those . . . paper towels. Yes! Those paper towels!" we say, delighted to have forced the brain to identify the object. Meanwhile our children stare at us like we've just landed from outer space. Okay, so it wasn't a rocket-science moment. Much more like oatmeal. Mushy, bland, blasé thinking. But thankfully, these moments do not define us. They are given to us to entertain our families, and so we may comfort our grandmothers that their forgetfulness is nothing compared to ours.

I love the honesty and self-deprecating humor of author and speaker Sue Buchanan. When she gets up to speak she enlightens her audiences straight away. "I may as well tell you, because you'll figure it out anyway: I'm not that deep." Her audience laughs. "I'm shallow," she says, and they laugh again. "But I'm deep for a shallow person." As she says in her book *Duh-votions*, "But here's what's *really* funny! Afterward a lot of people—I'm talkin' a *lot* of people—come up to me and say, 'I'm just like you. I'm shallow too! I've just never admitted it before.'"[1]

But there's more to Sue than she lets on. She says,

> I've spent the better part of a lifetime playing the role of an intellectually challenged dumb blonde, not only in everyday actions, but spiritually as well . . . (then) sixteen years ago, I had cancer and the experience changed my life—my heart. I began to ask questions and—Surprise! Surprise!—I've been *thinking* occasionally! I feel as if I've been spiritually asleep from birth and have been waking up in increasingly larger increments; awake longer each time.[2]

Good for her! It takes effort to think and live life really awake, an effort we should all be making.

It is so easy in our visual culture to engage in mind-numbing entertainment, routine work, repetitive chores, and passive activities that it's possible to go for long periods of time *without really thinking*. Certainly without thinking deeply. Therein lies the danger and the challenge. Striving to think beyond the surface and immediacy of life and attempting to expand my mind is one way I fight going south, one avenue in which I work hard to cultivate growth while praying for God to increase my capacity. I want to encourage you to live your life as a woman who thinks deeply!

But what is thinking, really, and aren't some people just better at it than others? *The Art of Thinking* puts it this way: "Thinking is any mental activity that helps formulate or solve a problem, make a decision, or fulfill a desire to understand. It is a searching for answers, a reaching for meaning . . . with mental activities including careful observation, remembering, wondering, imagining, inquiring, interpreting, evaluation, and judging."[3] The challenge is to search for answers beyond "what's for dinner" and to reach for meaning beyond why the dryer eats 47 percent of all sock mates.

Thankfully, thinking well can be learned. "Any notion that better thinking is intrinsically unlearnable and unteachable is nothing but a lazy fallacy, entertained only by those who have never taken the trouble to consider just how a practical job of thinking is really done."[4] True, some have more talent or are faster learners than others, but thinking well is largely a matter of habit, a habit that we can develop if we choose. "Research proves that the qualities of mind it takes to think well . . . can be mastered by anyone. . . . Most important, it proves that you don't need a high IQ to be a good thinker."[5]

The Fallacies of Our Excuses

Why is expanding our minds such a challenge? Well, we have a few cultural thought patterns that either influence us incognito or that we willingly fling about as excuses.

"I don't have time." Life is as busy as we make it, and we do find time in our days for the things we value. We would never say we're too busy to eat or sleep consistently; why

then is it okay to say we're too busy to learn? It's not. For a mentally growing woman it is vital; learning is nourishment for the brain.

The gray matter's not what it used to be. After all, I'm . . . aging. "Big deal!" I say. We've been aging since the moment we were born. People point to the exponential learning potential of the young and to the declining learning ability of the aging and come to the above excuse, uh, conclusion that our brains aren't what they once were. On my twenty-fifth birthday a friend told me, "Well, it's all downhill now. From today forward your cells are dying instead of growing." *Au contraire!* New brain research is revising the traditional view of how the brain ages. "Evidence clearly shows that the brain doesn't have to go into a steep decline as we get older," write Lawrence Katz and Manning Rubin in *Keep Your Brain Alive.* "In fact, in 1998, a team of American and Swedish scientists demonstrated for the first time that *new brain cells are generated in adult humans.*"[6] And in the book *How to Think Like Leonardo da Vinci,* author Michael Gelb writes, "Actually the average brain can improve with age. Our neurons are capable of making increasingly complex new connections throughout our lives."[7]

"I'm not very smart." This thinking mirrors the problem I discussed in chapter 3—"Your pot's too small." We think we can only learn so much, but God, who increases our capacity, does this with our minds as well. Want proof? A common belief for years was that intelligence was hardwired into us, fixed at birth. While we do have genetic preferences and talents, research has shown that we can improve our IQ with training and that our genes aren't the only factor determining how smart we are. A review of more than two hundred IQ studies found that "genes account for no more than 48 percent of IQ. Fifty-two percent is a function of

prenatal care, environment, and education."[8] And to that I add habit and effort, as we'll see in a moment.

"I finished school." To the person who thinks learning is what we do *until* we get a diploma, I want to send a T-shirt emblazoned with this:

"The truly educated never graduate!"

One of my top personal goals and delights (as well as goals for my children) is to be a lifelong learner.

"Why spend time on intellectualism when spirituality is what matters?" This is a spiritual-sounding excuse, but it is devoid of logic. It's like saying "Why bother to eat when spiritual food is what's important?" Some critics call efforts at higher learning cultural snobbery; I call that thinking a fallacy. All learning should be approached with balance and right motives, as well as humility, love, and an awe of God (for "knowledge makes arrogant, but love edifies" [1 Cor. 8:1]). Yet there is nothing spiritual about shunning aspirations to think well and expand our minds. I'm not aware of God giving brownie points for the stupidest believer. Christians get far too much criticism for checking their brains at the door of faith as it is. Counter this false perception! Impact your part of the world by demonstrating that faith and reason are *not* mutually exclusive.

"But I'm just a _____ (mom, store clerk, etc.)." To this I say, "And your point is . . . ?" No matter what our calling and vocation in life is, we can and should challenge our thinking and fill our mental storehouse as long as we take up space and breathe.

The Problems of an Unchallenged Mind

There are many problems with an unchallenged mind, not the least being ignorance, but here are some of the top reasons why mental stagnation is dangerous, unattractive, unwise, and an otherwise bad idea.

An unchallenged mind slows down mental processing. How our brains process—the speed at which we can take in new information, store it, retrieve it, and output it—depends in large part on the amount of exercise we give it. "Use it or lose it" is true. Low to no mental challenge stunts our processing ability.

An unchallenged mind makes us boring. Sad, but true. There is an observable correlation between someone who is happy in their limited thinking and the number of people who clamor to sit next to them at dinner parties. How long do you want to chat with someone who is only capable of discussing the weather and garbanzo beans? However, people who work at thinking and grapple with ideas simply have more to say than those who do not, and consequently have more influence.

With an unchallenged mind we risk becoming unfulfilled and discontent. An unchallenged mind may just wake up one day, take a look around at the oatmeal environment, and spit out little thoughts like, *So is this all there is?* That dangerous line leads to discontent with yourself, your purpose, and the people in your life; left unchecked or handled in an ungodly way, it can be a stepping stone to sinful or destructive behavior.

With an unchallenged mind we take our children south with us by example. We may think we slide by unnoticed in a state of mental-growth apathy, but our children perceive far more than we imagine. If dinner conversation is limited to the latest video we've seen, if we never engage in conversations about things that matter, if we talk about people or things rather than ideas, or if we seldom discuss things we are learning, we are placing our children at a great disadvantage.

176

With an unchallenged mind we waste potential God gives us. Long-term complacency is an affront to God. It's like being given a mansion and choosing to live in the garage. So much potential, so much beauty, so much space wasted. What might God do with us and through us if we committed to letting him increase our mental capacity and began working with him to do our part in that process?

With an unchallenged mind we limit our capacity to know God. This is the gravest of all the problems—an utter waste. We already see through a glass dimly, so why further obscure the vision? Yes, God is found in the shallow recesses of life, the gospel is simple and clear, and we are to have a childlike faith, but how much better it is to improve the depth of our thinking and go as deep with God as we can.

The Benefits of Expanding the Mind

When we fill our minds, work at improving our processing and increasing our mental capacity, and pray for God to stretch us beyond our capability, wonderful things happen. Seeking mental challenges and purposeful input results in greater processing ability, a greater depth of thinking, and the possibility of greater depths of knowing God. While I do want more knowledge about God, and find that studying Christology (the study of Christ) is vastly fruitful, the goal isn't merely to gain information. The facts benefit and support our faith and add reason to our repertoire, but what I want is a mind that is enabled to understand, know, and love God more each day.

Also, when we expand our minds, we become more interesting and available in community. Oh sure, it's fun to sparkle at a party, but the point of our existence is to be the hands and feet of Christ. It may not take much mental

177

ability to serve in a soup kitchen, but what if God calls you to run the soup kitchen or defend your faith with reason and logic while you are there? What if he calls you to do something beyond what you are capable of now? What if he wants you to help others with something you know that they do not? The more we think, the more we have to say; and the more we have to say that is insightful and meaningful, the more we are able to engage others. And that just might open the door for conversations about God and his kingdom that we wouldn't have had if we'd just discussed, say, lemon meringue pie.

Our brains are tools we can use for God's purposes, just as we let him use our bodies and our service. A brain that functions well, that is regularly filled with useful information, can also help others. Because we should seek to grow to give, we can *expect* God to provide opportunities for us to share our knowledge and insights with others in a way that will help them. For example, I had a minor health problem once that prompted me to do a bit of research that I found quite helpful. The next week I "happened" to come in contact with a woman who was in the same situation and was terrified that she was in mortal danger. I shared my information with her, and the next day she called, physically relieved and no longer fearful. I've seen God put people in my path like this so often that now I sort of expect it.

The opposite of the problems of an unchallenged mind that I've listed become the benefits of one that's filled and challenged: Our processing improves, we're not boring, we are more fulfilled, we have more to give our children as we stimulate them with our own stimulated thinking and as they observe our mental growth. The more we know, the more we can teach them. The deeper we think, the more we can teach them to do likewise. One of the easiest and most pleasurable ways to fill and challenge your mind, engage in deep thinking, and involve your children in this process is to read aloud to them. Read quality literature, children's classics, using guidebooks like *Honey for a Child's Heart* by Gladys Hunt or *Books Children Love* by Elizabeth Wilson, to help you locate the richest, most engaging literature. I've read aloud to toddlers and teenagers, tucking away cherished memories amidst the learning.

To me, learning and discovering new information, new ways of thinking, ideas I'd never considered before, is one of the most wonderful things God lets me do. Learning excites me. It gives me a little glimmer of excitement for heaven, because I envision it as more than just an endless church service; I see unlimited learning and discovery of the things of God and his creation. Expanding my mind in this life lets me see as much as I can of God through my dim glass, and it increases my potential and my capacity to know him.

The Focus of Our Learning

Before jumping into the fascinating research on how the brain functions and how we can improve our thinking, let's go back to God's Word on the subject. What should our learning focus on according to Scripture?

The knowledge of God. "So that you will walk in a manner worthy of the Lord, to please Him in all respects, bearing fruit in every good work and increasing in the knowledge of God" (Col 1:10). Or put another way:

> We haven't stopped praying for you, asking God to give you wise minds and spirits attuned to his will, and so acquire a thorough understanding of the ways in which God works. We pray that you'll live well for the Master, making him proud of

you as you work hard in his orchard. As you learn more and more how God works, you will learn how to do *your* work.

Colossians 1:10

We are also to "grow in the grace and knowledge of our Lord and Savior Jesus Christ" (2 Peter 3:18).

What pleases God. Scripture says that we should walk as children of the light, "trying to learn what is pleasing to the Lord" (Eph. 5:10).

The Word of God. The way to do the above, to increase our knowledge of God and to learn what pleases him, is to study his Word. Other learning in our lives should come second.

> Be diligent to present yourself approved to God as a workman who does not need to be ashamed, accurately handling the word of truth. . . . All Scripture is inspired by God and profitable for teaching, for reproof, for correction, for training in righteousness; so that the man of God may be adequate, equipped for every good work.
>
> 2 Timothy 2:15; 3:16–17

When we make a decision to learn more about the things of God and embark on the task of expanding our minds, it can be a bit overwhelming. There's so much to learn! But we can take comfort that God is our source of all knowledge and is our teacher: "Even He who teaches man knowledge" (Ps. 94:10) and "For the LORD gives wisdom; from His mouth come knowledge and understanding" (Prov. 2:6). As I dedicate myself to learning all that I can, I pray that God will make me ever mindful that my real goal in this department goes beyond knowledge and understanding. My goal is to gain wisdom, as the first four chapters of Proverbs teach, because knowledge is better than gold and wisdom is better than jewels, incomparable to anything else we could desire (Prov. 8:10–11).

Growing Our Brains

I'm glad to be living in an age when research shows that our brains can grow beyond childhood, that aging doesn't have to be feared, that strokes and head injuries can be treated, and that for those who are going to get dementia and Alzheimer's, symptoms can be delayed. The brain has far more plasticity than previously believed. Studies show that educated people are less likely to show symptoms of Alzheimer's disease because intellectual activity stimulates brain tissue that compensates for disease-damaged tissue. In some stroke victims with areas of the brain permanently damaged, new pathways can be created to resume function of the damaged areas.

In *Building a Better Brain,* Daniel Golden writes,

> Individuals have some control over how healthy and alert their brains remain as the years go by. Recent research suggests that stimulating the mind with mental exercise may cause brain cells, called neurons, to branch wildly causing millions of additional connections, or synapses, between brain cells. Think of it, says Arnold Scheibel, director of UCLA's Brain Research Institute, as a computer with a bigger memory board: "You can do more things more quickly."[9]

The key then is to find ways to switch neurons on and grow dendrites, and we do that by keeping our minds active. Other ways to grow new connections include doing logic problems, crosswords, puzzles, brainteasers, and memory exercises. Also, try to use all your senses (vision, touch, taste, smell, hearing, and "emotions"). According to *Keep Your Brain Alive*, just seeing a rose activates a small number of neural pathways, but seeing, smelling, and touching it activates *more* pathways. When you meet someone, don't just use sight to identify the person, use all your senses. Think, *Thinning hair, glasses, hand feels like a damp rag, smells like a smokehouse, voice sounds like a bullfrog.* This makes it easier to recall the name of the person later. If you're over thirty-five, encourage yourself with this:

> Adopting the strategies of forming multisensory associations when the brain is still at or near its peak performance—in the forties and fifties—builds a bulwark against some of the inevitable loss of processing power later in life. If your network of associations is very large, it's like having a very tightly woven net, and the loss of a few threads isn't going to let much fall through.[10]

Another major dendrite grower is the unexpected. So actively experience the unfamiliar. Novelty turns on the brain and increases cortical activity in varied areas and strengthens synapses. If you work with words all day, you might paint or draw. If you are artistic, try dancing. If you are a numbers person, take up a musical instrument. Novel activity grows dendrites and enhances our minds.

A Plan for Expanding Your Mind

- Know the value and benefits of learning and working your mind. They can be great motivators.
- Recognize your obstacles to growing mentally. When you encounter them, renew your mind with positive thoughts about learning, and take captive all lies and excuses.

182

- Decide to act.
- Pray for God's direction in the things he would have you apply your mind to and the knowledge he desires for you to acquire.
- Rediscover curiosity. It's a hallmark of great minds, because they ask questions. The author of *How to Think Like Leonardo da Vinci* says, "The questions that 'engage our thought' on a daily basis reflect our life purpose and influence the quality of our lives."[11]
- Improve your ability to communicate what you are learning—your ability to speak, write, and persuade with logic and clarity.
- Increase your exposure to ideas through words and interesting people. Passive entertainment does not do this.
- Read books about learning to think well, such as James W. Sire's excellent work *Habits of the Mind: Intellectual Life as a Christian Calling.*
- Create a learning plan to continue your self-education.

1. *Schedule time daily* for your own learning. Start with half an hour, mornings if possible, or at your peak concentration time of day if you can fit it into your lifestyle.
2. *Improve your reading.* It's a key to reasoning. Os Guinness writes "Believe in the supreme value of words and their inescapable importance for the life of the mind and the human spirit."[12] One of the most important aspects of remembering what you read and gleaning ideas and reasoning from it is to ask questions of the author and respond to the ideas. Mark up the book. Underline. Highlight. Ask questions and make comments in the margins. Record favorite pas-

sages and page numbers or main ideas gleaned and your responses and impressions to the material in the front or back pages. This is something that C. S. Lewis did and that Mortimer Adler teaches in *How to Read a Book*, a book that I highly recommend.

You can improve your reading speed dramatically simply by concentrating. "Merely focusing more intently on what you read catapults your speed and comprehension light years ahead."[13] One experiment showed that volunteers who did this, while still reading every word and striving for comprehension, improved their speed by 25 to 50 percent without losing any understanding. Don't subvocalize (form words with your mouth or say words under your breath). Your brain can take in information faster than you can mouth words. Don't backtrack (your brain gets it more often than not), and practice reading a phrase at a time instead of a word at a time. Preread a book by looking at the title, back cover, table of contents, index, and then skim the highlights of the chapters before diving into page 1.

Read as much as you can. And there's joy found in rereading quality literature, because we always see something new. Why? "When you reread a classic," says Clifton Fadiman in *Any Number Can Play,* "you do not see more in the book than you did before; you see more in you than there was before." It's a sign of our growth.[14]

3. *Pick a high-interest topic.* Choose something that highly interests you, sticking to one topic at a time for a period of time. What do you wish you knew more about? Where are the holes in your education? Do you know the flow of history? Study it chronologically and read primary sources, biographies, histori-

cal novels, and literature written in the time period you're studying.

Ditch textbooks—they're the reason most people dislike history. Start working on a "great books" list with the help of Cliffs Notes or some of the great guidebooks available for an overview. I love using *Invitation to the Classics* by Louise Cowan and Os Guinness. C. S. Lewis said we need books that will correct the characteristic mistakes of our own period, so he recommended reading one old book after every new, or at the least one old after three new. It's never too late to begin the education you wish you'd had!

4. *Keep a learning journal or notebook.* I learned this great idea from Susan Wise Bauer, one of the authors of *The Well-Trained Mind.* This is a huge key to absorbing and remembering what you are learning. As you read and study, write down facts, outlines, questions, and your responses to what you are studying. You can accumulate a series of notebooks over time that Bauer says will chronicle your intellectual journey. Reread them every six months.

5. *Subscribe to a journal* (literary, trade, general interest) that interests you. Make notes, file articles, and note books others are reading.

Improve Your Memory, Brain Power, and Learning Potential

Here are a few of my favorite tips for increasing our learning, processing, and remembering, gleaned from many sources. As I said before, concentrating can improve our reading speed, but it can also greatly improve our memory. Be interested and vividly attend to what you are trying to learn or remember. "It may be hard to believe, but just paying attention can double your brain power. In a sense, this system underlies all the other memory doublers science has developed."[15] Concentrating is simply overcoming (not preventing) distractions. "The secret of efficient thinkers is not that they experience fewer distractions but that they have learned to deal with them more quickly and more effectively than inefficient thinkers do."[16] Since concentration can double your brainpower, it makes sense that by dividing our attention we cut our brainpower in half. That sounds scary for us divergent-thinking, multitasking women. While we have the ability to multitask, we can also concentrate on doing just one thing at a time when we really want to maximize our mental ability.

Practice visual and verbal mnemonics for better recall. Visualize what you're trying to remember or give yourself verbal clues or codes like ROY G. BIV, an acronym for the colors of the spectrum (red, orange, yellow, etc.), or "Harry-not" to remember the name of the bald man you just met. Or try this "memory glue," as one source calls this commonsense approach: Believe you will remember it. Tell yourself to remember it. Mentally review what you want to remember the next day to reinforce it.

Organize the information. We must have a context into which to put new information, and the context must be relevant to us so we can recall it. "Organization helps in two ways," says the author of *Your Memory*. "It structures what is being learnt, so that recalling a fragment of information is likely to make the rest accessible; and it relates newly learnt material to what has gone before, which means that the richer your existing knowledge structure is the easier it is to comprehend and remember new material."[17] To organize new information, relate the material to yourself and your own interests as much as possible. As William James once said, "One who thinks over his experiences most and weaves them into systematic relations with each other will be the one with the best memory."

Then there's the total time hypothesis, which means that how much we learn depends on the time we spend learning. Memory tricks are great, but we must put in the time—just not all at once. Our brains learn better when we input information with the right frequency, intensity, and duration. I learned this from the National Academy of Child Development, which helped me develop a program to work with my son. For optimum learning we need high frequency (input information often), with lots of intensity, but of a short duration. It's a great way to get math facts into kids, and it has carryover to our learning as well.

What a comfort to know the brain actually learns better this way than in long, tiring sessions. We can make use of all the intervals of life, the waiting times, to learn. For this reason I carry note cards and a book almost everywhere and keep them by my bed. I jot down things I don't want to forget, put short notes on cards to study while waiting in line or at doctor appointments, and read in snatches. I hate to be caught bookless.

Some experts suggest self-rewards as motivation for learning new things, but I find that the discovery is reward enough. A better strategy is to learn in order to teach, because what we study in order to teach others is far better understood and remembered than what we learn just for ourselves. Share with a friend, teach a class, teach your children, write an article or a book. This is one reason I write—it's a key to my growth!

Here are some additional tips to improve your ability to learn. Move and fuel your body to give your brain what it needs; exercise supplies the brain with oxygen, and eating well gives it nutrients. Find your peak time of day and the best conditions for you, be it total quiet, some noise, or classical music (which, by the way, does positively impact brain function—the so-called "Mozart effect"). Some researchers point to our Optimum Learning State, or "flow" or peak performance times, when we learn easily, joyfully, and quickly. To be able to do that all the time would be wonderful, right? Practicing slow, deep breathing and relaxation before learning or using what you've learned can get you closer to this state.

Gatekeeping

Here's a short bit on something I feel strongly about that has nothing to do with expanding our minds but everything to do with being good stewards of them. We must be careful guardians of what we allow to enter our minds: ideas, written words, spoken words, music, and especially visual images. We must be vigilant gatekeepers, guarding against the entry of things that pollute and distort, which means we must often be willing to go against cultural norms of acceptability. We need to use spiritual discernment, developing sensitivity to what is often culturally acceptable. Saying "Those things don't bother me" may be true, but we should ask, "Is it right?" I've heard it said that what we sometimes choose for entertainment, God calls an abomination. Also, some things that enter our minds have a way of never leaving; some images that hit our brains become like photographs stored indefinitely, whether we want them there or not. The problem is that they can come flying out of our mental file drawers when we least expect it; if they are violent or polluted images, this is unsettling and destructive. I still have vivid recall of a nightmare I had when I was seven and a horror movie scene I accidentally saw when I was eight.

Be cautious in your gatekeeping, for yourself and especially for your children. Paul said in Philippians 4:8 that we should think on whatever is lovely, good, excellent, and worthy. That's far easier to do when we carefully guard all that enters our minds.

Portraits of Learning

You may wonder if real women really have time to devote to developing the mind. Absolutely, if the desire is strong enough. Years ago I read of a woman who studied and became an expert on Japanese diplomacy or some such thing so she could speak intelligently with her husband and his business colleagues on the subject. In another instance, a dear friend of mine began to be consumed with questions about her faith. She knew *what* she believed, but the whys and their application began to trouble her. She started reading for answers to her questions, investigating church history to better understand the grand scheme of our great heritage and the arguments and defenses made by some of the church fathers. Her curiosity and subsequent delight with what she was discovering led her through a two-year theological boot camp of reading Scripture and studying the minds of John Calvin, Martin Luther, and others. It changed her. I saw the effect of her learning as her approach to apologetics was strengthened; her conversations became peppered with her new information, and the application of that knowledge impacted her life. Her quest for information and truth continues as one avenue of study opens doors to another; she keeps on learning, growing, and finding ways to mentally organize the material and relate it to her life. She's discovered that finding pegs on which to hang the new ideas, thoughts, and knowledge is important to help her recall and utilize the material. It's been the biggest intellectual and spiritual journey of her life, and I feel privileged to have witnessed so much growth in her. And yet, her study time came between laundry and shopping and work, as she was a widowed mom with three kids.

An order of nuns in Mankato, Minnesota, who are part of a brain research study, are proving the value of brain exercise. Their average age is eighty-five, a large number of them are over ninety, and they don't seem to get Alzheimer's or dementia symptoms as early or as badly as the general public. Brain workouts are a lifestyle for them—they do puzzles, brainteasers, attend current-events seminars and discuss the topics afterward. They also regularly write letters and spiritual meditations. One sister taught until she was ninety-seven, and another volunteered at the front desk at age ninety-nine. One professor who has studied the nuns for years found that "those who earn college degrees, who teach, who constantly challenge their minds, live longer than less-educated nuns who clean rooms or work in the kitchen. He suspects the difference lies in how they use their heads."[18] We can still clean and work in the kitchen as moms everywhere do, but we must also use our heads daily.

My greatest intellectual challenge thus far has not been college or experiential learning in my broadcasting days, but has been embarking on a journey of classical education for my children and myself. This journey reflects an attempt to immerse them, as Wes Callihan writes in *A Guide to the Great Books*, "in the thoughts and events of the past as the primary means of learning to deal with the present, and to implant in them a deep love and critical *appreciation of the written and spoken word as the vehicle of the ideas* that shape culture"[19] (emphasis mine).

Always a lover of words and great literature and frustrated with the compartmentalized subjects in schools, I was drawn to the idea of a classical education incorporating aspects of the trivium—the grammar, logic, and rhetoric stages of a child's learning. As Dorothy Sayers said in "The Lost Tools of Learning," a speech given at Oxford in 1947, "Although we often succeed in teaching our pupils 'subjects,' we fail lamentably on the whole in teaching them how to think: They learn everything, except the art of learning." As I go on this journey with my children, I find that I too am learning to think and how to learn, for as Sayers also said, the sole true end of education is simply to teach men how to learn for themselves.

This learning has taken us into the world of the great books, the classics, and is allowing us to take part in the "great conversation"—the examination of ideas about God, good and evil, who we are, why we're here, and other issues important to man. These are the concepts and questions dealt with by writers, poets, scientists, philosophers, historians, and others across millennia. Oh sure, it's daunting at times, but the benefits of such reading help shape us. Louis Cowan, coeditor of *Invitation to the Classics*, says these books seize our imaginations and summon us to belief.

In the eighteenth and nineteenth centuries, American common people had a great knowledge of the Bible, Shakespeare, and liberal arts and had high language skills. Early Harvard entrants were expected to enter college with a working knowledge of Latin or Greek. However, such learning is challenged today because we live in a world of two extremes, the elite knowledge of specialization and the dumbing down of America. This produces information technologists with multiple degrees alongside others with sluggish thinking and language inspired by a culture saturated in all things visual—the "Dumb and Dumber" effect.

So at some level, with baby steps, perhaps, I fight back—for the minds of my children. For my own mind. And because life is interesting. Intellectual improvement is a targeted arrow in the battle to keep from going south. It's one of the most challenging tasks I've ever undertaken, as Latin and logic texts and Augustine and Austen and A. A. Milne litter our home and fight for equal time with the laundry. If I only accomplish a fraction of what I desire for my children, and only learn a bit of what I'd like to personally, we will still be better off than if we'd never tried, for my love of learning propels me, for my sake and theirs. And I know that five years from now, I will not be the same person I am today; I will have grown.

Your brain is so much better than you think . . . God made it. Fight going south by picking up a crossword or a classic, doing something new outside of your usual abilities that access your senses and makes you think. Change a routine, decide to study something you like . . . and watch your capacity increase and your mind expand.

> For wisdom will enter your heart and knowledge will be pleasant to your soul.
>
> Proverbs 2:10

11

Disneyland or LaLa Land
Handling Our Emotions and Our Wills

M en decide far more problems by hate, love, lust, rage, sorrow, joy, hope, fear, illusion, or some other inward emotion, than by reality, authority, any legal standard, judicial precedent, or statute." Cicero, the classical orator, politician, and philosopher, said this over two thousand years ago, but it could easily be said today. Our emotions permeate our being; they are woven into the fiber of who we are, influencing how we feel, how we communicate, how we solve problems, even how we live. At times our emotions can yank us onto a wild ride, like a daredevil friend who pulls us onto a roller coaster with breathtaking highs, stomach-flipping dips, and even a few loops. We revel in the thrill of the ride but usually end up at some point longing for the peaceful lazy river instead. If we're not careful, and we find ourselves *living* in the grip of an emotionally charged existence, we might just head south, from Disneyland to LaLa land.

I love being a woman. I cherish my emotional nature and the fact that I'm made in the image of God. I love that God understands emotion; in Scripture he reveals his compassion, wrath, indescribable love for us, and joy. Isaiah 60:5 (NIV) says this about God: "Your heart will throb and swell with joy." I also love that much of the fruit of the Spirit listed in Galatians 5 is exhibited in the emotional aspect of our character. Love, joy, peace, gentleness . . . we *feel* these things as well as live them. We are able to feel and experience so many beautiful emotions: inexpressible joy at the birth of a child; exhilaration when we fall in love; utter peacefulness in moments of quiet family time; compassion and empathy when a loved one shares a burden; laughter, the medicine for our souls. Why, some of us are moved to tears through books, movies, and even commercials! I think about all these emotions, and I'm grateful to God for creating us with the ability to feel, which adds color, depth, richness, and beauty to our lives.

One of my friends was recently reminded of the value of our emotional nature. She heard author Daniel Goleman speak on his concept of emotional intelligence, a sort of intelligence that enhances the ability and wisdom to communicate well, socially and relationally. In his book *Emotional Intelligence* he wrote,

> People with greater certainty about their feelings are better pilots of their lives, having a surer sense of how they really feel about personal decisions from whom to marry to what job to take. . . . Emotionally intelligent women, by contrast [to purely high-IQ women], tend to be assertive and express their feelings directly, and feel positive about themselves; life holds meaning for them.[1]

194

After my friend and her husband heard Goleman speak about the practical value of emotions and their worth in our lives, she said her husband gained a heightened respect for her and a more positive understanding of the emotional side of her personality.

However, as we well know, not all of our emotions are positive. The backseat of our emotional ride is steep, dark, and filled with curves that rattle our brains. A husband abandons his promises and commits adultery, leaving his wife in the wake of suffocating hurt. A young girl's abortion leaves a riptide of regret. A previously infertile woman revels in a new pregnancy, but a miscarriage drop-kicks her into waves of lingering sadness. A woman waits on pins and needles for a week to find out if the test indicates cancer or not; each day is a year long and her nights are filled with mind-numbing fear. A stressed young mother with three preschoolers and an absent husband finds her coping skills scarce and yelling episodes increasingly habitual; anger has her by the throat. Another woman's husband suddenly dies. She's consumed with too many emotions to count. These women's feelings of hurt, regret, sadness, fear, anger, and grief are but a few of the many emotions that rattle our lives.

Meanwhile, each of these women still faces everyday life. The sun rises and brings new circumstances wrought with even more emotion to deal with. They find themselves emotionally overloaded, looking for escape from a ride gone awry.

The Problems of Emotional Overload

There are several problems with allowing ourselves to live a life that too easily or often crosses the line from emotional balance to emotional overload (including the fact that our emotions trickle down into our children's lives). The first problem is that our emotions control *us* instead of us controlling our emotions. We wait for the circumstance, then yield to the ensuing emotion. We feel like victims of our emotions, powerless to change our feelings.

This leads to the second problem. Sin. Allowing ourselves to just feel whatever we feel, unchecked, is dangerous and unbiblical. For example, we feel justified in our anger because we were wronged, so we fail to forgive, in spite of the scriptural directive to do so. Or we wallow in self-pity, not recognizing it as a form of pride. When we scream or get physical in anger directed at people, we are ignoring the Scriptures that say to be angry but sin not, or to consider one another's interests ahead of our own. Anxiety over money or clothes (or whatever) violates the command to be anxious for nothing, but in everything to trust God. And so on. When our emotions rule us, we are not exercising self-control.

Another problem with living too much in the emotional realm is that emotions are a poor indicator of reality. How we *feel* about a matter often has little bearing on the facts because, simply put, emotions easily change. A girl likes one boy this month, another one the next month. We storm over to confront a friend in the throes of anger, when if we'd calmed down and examined the facts, we'd have felt differently in the morning. We were up for four hours with a sick child, and stumble, exhausted and blue, through the day, but after a good night's sleep, all feels right with the world again.

The most dangerous aspect of living too emotionally is that sheer emotions can lead us away from truth. After all, as Scripture says, "The heart is desperately wicked, who can know it?" When our focus is on how we feel, we often forget or ignore what God's Word says. For example, when our lives take a turn we don't like, we can sometimes feel like God let us down, that his care for us wasn't what it should have been. But the truth is that he loves us and desires our good, always.

Emotional overload has another problem. It can lead us away from reason. When we are being led by out-of-control emotions, we often fail to apply reason, logic, and clear thought to situations. It is not a woman's emotional nature that gives her the bad reputation of being moody and controlled by feelings. It is the out-of-control, unreasoning acts that do.

When you feel emotionally overwhelmed, remember this: We are not helpless victims of our emotions unless we choose to remain in their captivity! God gives us tools to handle them, and also the Holy Spirit within us to help us be the balanced women we want to be. Let's look at some of those tools.

Handling Our Emotions

1. Recognize Physical Reasons for Emotional Overload

Inadequate rest, poor health, and hormone levels are physical symptoms that can trigger an emotional response. Sleep deprivation and a compromised body can impair our thinking and our ability to maintain an emotional even keel, as discussed in the chapter about rest, so be sure you get enough sleep and down time. And most women are fully aware of the link between hormone levels and emotions, from PMS symptoms, to the "baby blues," to emotional surges after a hysterectomy or menopause.

In *Emotional Phases of a Woman's Life*, author Jean Lush likens the emotional parallels of our menstrual cycle to the

197

ebb and flow of the ocean tide. She says we can be "calm and serene with gentle swells one day, then hurricane gales and tidal waves the next. Sometimes we wonder if we'll survive."[2] Many women find that when their estrogen and progesterone levels drop, either during their monthly cycle or menopause, so do their drive, ambition, and mood. I echo Jean's advice: "If your emotions overrun reason and become too much for you to handle—and some women with premenstrual syndrome fall into that category—medical intervention may be necessary."[3] These are often physical symptoms that can be relieved by a qualified health provider's care. And sometimes medication can be a temporary boost to help us make the other necessary changes in our lives.

2. Know Your Personal Danger Signals

Pay attention to the triggers that routinely set you off emotionally. Be aware of the number of hours of sleep you need, what activities and interests you need to participate in, what things you should avoid, and the pace of life at which you best operate.

I used to be unaware of some very obvious triggers in my life. I'd find myself getting tense and easily frustrated, not recognizing my cyclical emotionality and the hormonal cause. One day, my observant husband said, "Lin, don't you *ever* look at a calendar?" I did from that day on, which enabled me to be proactive during that time to better control my emotions. I got extra sleep, avoided problematic issues or decision making if I could, and allowed more margin in my day. (The french fry splurge then didn't hurt either.)

We not only need to be aware of the things that ignite us emotionally, but also to be aware of areas in which we are emotionally out of balance yet complacent about it. Just as a person with allergies can get so used to the discomfort that they perceive it as normal, we can get so used to the blues or irritability or other negative emotions that we lose the desire to be fully alive as God designed. Praying for an awareness of emotional triggers and a nudge out of any complacency can help us better handle our emotions.

3. Apply Reason

Granted, some women tend to be more thoughtful while others are more emotional in nature, but all of us can choose to use the tool of reason to balance our emotions. Marya Mannes said, "The sign of intelligent people is their ability to control emotions by the application of reason." We can learn to respond more thoughtfully and logically to situations rather than just reacting emotionally. When we feel ourselves getting worked up more than we should, we need to step back, close our mouths, and think for a moment. What are the facts? What is the truth? Lay aside how you feel about the issue and think through it instead. Perhaps talk with your husband or a friend who is a good logical or linear thinker. Sometimes simply being aware of the need to separate how you feel about an issue from the facts at hand can help you apply reason and gain emotional balance.

And of course, when we apply reason and ponder truth, we need to be sure of the veracity of our source, not trusting our imaginations or emotions. Joni Eareckson Tada and Steven Estes write this in *When God Weeps:*

> But our imaginations about God aren't reliable—ancient speculations about the kind of birthday present he might like led cultures into human sacrifice. Nor can we simply trust our emotions about him—if we conceive of God as we'd like him to be, we're sure to recreate him in our

own image. We're liable to become like the people Paul described: "They are zealous for God, but their zeal is not based on knowledge" (Rom. 10:2).

The Bible is our only safe source of knowledge about God—and it requires thinking. God's persistent invitation in every age remains: "'Come now, let us *reason* together,' says the Lord" (Isa. 1:18).[4]

4. Train Emotional Habits

Haven't you noticed how we can get into emotional response habits? Like a toddler who develops the bad habit of screaming when she doesn't get her way, we can pick up certain habitual responses as well. Therefore, it's important we exercise that fruit of the Spirit, self-control, and train our emotions as best we can. C. S. Lewis wrote in *The Abolition of Man,*

> Without the aid of trained emotions the intellect is power-less against the animal organism. I had sooner play cards against a man who was quite skeptical about ethics, but bred to believe that "a gentleman does not cheat," than against an irreproachable moral philosopher who had been brought up among sharpers. . . . As the king governs by his executive, so Reason in man must rule the mere appetites by means of the "spirited element." The head rules the belly through the chest—the seat, as Alanus tells us, of Magnanimity, of *emotions organized by trained habit into stable sentiment.*[5]
>
> emphasis mine

Just as we correct tantrum-throwing toddlers and model the appropriate response to them, we can learn to correct ourselves, even taking a "time out" to avoid an emotional outburst if needed, and go to Scripture as our model for appropriate responses. When we're trying to train ourselves in a specific habit, we might ask someone close to us to help hold us accountable.

5. Apply Practical Helps

There are many practical steps we can take in handling our emotions. Don't forget the mind/body/spirit connection that we've already discussed. Getting enough natural light, rest, and exercise affects how we feel. Allow yourself time to dream, to think, and to partake in soul nourishment, which we'll discuss in the next chapter.

Give yourself diversions. If you are in the midst of grief or anger, sometimes a break from the situation can help you regain perspective. Give yourself permission to divert your mind for a time. That might be through creative endeavors, recreational activities, or a change of scenery. When you do this you're not ignoring reality, you're just temporarily relieving tensions and refreshing your mind. Jean Lush writes in *Women and Stress* that "locking on to problems until they're solved actually cripples our ability to find solutions and leaves us exhausted. Answers are more easily detected by an open, peaceful mind, rather than one that is hypervigilant and anxious."[6]

It also helps to maintain order in your environment. Order and touches of beauty have the wonderful ability to calm. When life is swirling about you and emotions are whirling within, living and working in an organized, pleasant environment refreshes the soul, calms the spirit and mind, and even creates energy.

Another practical step for handling emotions is to carefully guard your visual, auditory, mental, and relational input. As I recommended earlier, be a vigilant gatekeeper, limiting "pollution" in your life. Moral filth, evil, and unedifying garbage are just a mouse click, channel hop, radio frequency, or page away, and it's our responsibility to reject the junk, because it affects the way we feel and think. Yet when we immerse ourselves in positive input through the books we read, the people we associate with, the tapes we listen to, and so on, we are positively affected. These things become a part of who we are.

If you are going through emotional pain, allow yourself tears, time, and talking. The tears of pain contain toxins, so allowing yourself a good tear-letting is cleansing. Don't cry longer than you need to, but know that having a good cry can help you function better. Getting through emotional pain like grief just takes time, varying in length among individuals. Don't feel pressured to heal according to others' schedules. Let God take you through this journey in his timing. And finally, tap into the human connection when you are hurting. Talk with those who love you and who have the gift of listening deeply. We often process how we feel simply by talking things out. Nurturing relationships and a healthy support system are vital to our emotional health.

6. Know God's Truths

The above suggestions for handling our emotions well—recognizing physical symptoms, knowing personal danger signals, training the emotions, and applying reason and practical helps—are all helpful, but without this last point, they are hollow. Knowing what we believe, based on God's truths, is foundational to our emotional health. Emotions are not things we pick up and put down, they are woven into our being and are a byproduct of what we believe. We have to know what we believe, know the foundational truths of our faith, and make sure they align with God's Word, because our beliefs affect our actions, which in turn affect our feelings. We must take *everything* back to the character of God—our emotions, our problems, our struggles, our feelings. We must ask ourselves, "How does what I'm feeling square with what I know about God's character?" Here's an example of the importance our beliefs have on our feelings.

Let's hypothetically say I was terribly hurt by someone in the past. It was horrible and I came away from it believing I not only had been hurt by man, but had been abandoned by God. Because I believe God abandoned me when I needed him, I am left feeling utterly victimized and vulnerable, the logical counterpoint to such a belief. I've believed a lie (God left me) and abandoned a truth (God never leaves us or forsakes us). On the other hand, if I believe that I've been hurt by man but am still within the parameters of God's plan for me, and that dark moment in my life is a part of God's providence to grow me into his image, then I won't feel trapped in victimization. I can deal with the pain and find forgiveness and healing because I *believe* that God keeps his promises and uses all things in my life for good, to make me more like him.

We must know the promises God lovingly gives us in his Word, and we must believe them by an act of our faith. We must examine all things in light of God's character—that he is loving, compassionate, just, and desires our good. We must embrace the tandem truths from Psalms that God is both sovereign, ultimately in charge of everything, *and* good. His goodness without his sovereignty makes him a Santa Claus, and his sovereignty without his goodness makes him a dictator—and he is neither. The bottom line is that his character, his promises, and our belief in both through our faith means that God can always be trusted. We are not left to fall victim to our emotions; we can trust God completely and find balance and health in our beliefs.

This is a complex issue and not necessarily a natural thought pattern, but it's important. The next time you find yourself struggling with emotions you'd rather shake, ask yourself, "What lie am I believing or what truth am I failing to believe?" And, "Am I trusting God's sovereignty and goodness?" That leads to our surrender, our willingness to release our emotions, the outcome of their contributing circumstances, and our expectations to God. But that's better discussed in light of our will.

Conquering Our Will

So far in this book we've looked at how we can keep from going south in spirit, body, and in this section, the soul. Our will is one aspect of our souls, so let's turn to that now, but looking through a very narrow lens. Folks have been arguing over the issue of free will up and down the pages of history. Just taking a look at the chapter titles of R. C. Sproul's book *Willing to Believe: The Controversy Over Free Will* is a short history lesson on the subject: We are capable of obedience (Pelagius). We are incapable of obedience (Augustine). We are capable of cooperation (Semi-Pelagians). We are in bondage to sin (Martin Luther). We are voluntary slaves (John Calvin). We are free to believe (James Arminius). We are inclined to sin (Jonathan Edwards). In light of the theological magnitude of the issue of the will, this section is a mere morsel of a very big pie.

Perhaps one of you is reading along and you've just come to this section on conquering the will, and you think something like this:

What a wonderful and tough thing, our will. It's wonderful that God gave me a free will, but it's also tough. There seem

204

to be far too many times that I just can't muster up enough willpower in my life to do what I know I should. I often do things I don't want to do and fail to do things I should. I totally relate to Paul when he wrote in Romans 7 that he decides one way then acts in another, doing the thing he hates. That's the story of my life. I guess I just have to get serious about my willpower, with God's help, of course.

Who can argue with that, right? Free will *is* a great gift; God could have made us automatons, but he didn't. It *is* difficult to decide to do some things when we'd rather not. And we've probably been hearing the word *willpower* tossed about since we were children and our mothers went on that grapefruit and yogurt diet. That was the extent of my thinking on the subject and the Romans passage for a long time. But let's look a little closer.

What is the will exactly? Of course, everyone knows the general meaning, but to clarify the nuance, let's use Jonathan Edwards's definition in his classic writing, *The Freedom of the Will*, which, incidentally, R. C. Sproul called the greatest theological work ever written. Edwards says:

> And therefore I observe, that the *Will* (without any metaphysical refining) is, *That by which the mind chooses any thing*. The faculty of the will, is that power, or principle of mind, by which it is capable of *choosing:* an act of the will is the same as an act of choosing or choice. So that by whatever names we call the act of the Will, choosing, refusing, approving, disapproving, liking, disliking, embracing, rejecting, determining, directing, commanding, forbidding, inclining, or being averse, being pleased or displeased with; all may be reduced to this of *choosing*.[7]

When we like cheeseburgers and dislike tofu, or command that the bathroom be cleaned and forbid eating crackers in bed, we are choosing and, therefore, are exercising our wills. Simple enough. But back to the above issue. Why in the world do we so often do things that we don't want to do?

We don't.

What? you may think. *Of course I do. I go to work and I don't want to. I drive carpool and I don't want to. I even passed on the cheesecake last night, and I sure didn't want to do that.* Okay, true enough on the surface, but here's a startling thought that may impact our view of our wills.

We always do what we *most* want to do.

I didn't say we always do what we *like* to do, but what we *want* to do the most at a given moment. The difference lies in our motivation. We may not like to go to work, but we go because we want to keep the kids in a Christian school. The consequences of not going to work are too high. We might not want to drive carpool, but we do it because there's no bus service for the school and we want to drive the kids *more* than we want them in the school that has a bus service. We don't think we want to give up the cheesecake, but we do because we want to stay on our current eating plan more than we want to eat it. Feeling better and losing weight is what we want *most* at that given moment. Or when we dig into that cheesecake when we've vowed to cut out sugar, we want our craving satisfied more than we want the benefits of refusing it. We always do what we *most* want to do.

The reason for this is our motivation. Edwards puts it this way: "It is that motive, which, as it stands in view of the mind, is the strongest, that determines the will."[8] I'm beginning to understand this. For years I'd get up in the morning, prepare to homeschool my children, and think, *I really don't want to do this.* I'd picture my friends whose children got on the bus each day while they sipped coffee in a quiet house and worked without interruption. Oh, I have plenty of wonderful moments in the endeavor of teaching my kids, but for me, home education has always been at a great personal sacrifice. I certainly never thought I was doing what I most wanted to do.

But then my thinking changed. My flesh, my desires, wanted peace, quiet, and a bit of solitude in which to write. Madeleine L'Engle once wrote that it's very difficult for a woman to be a writer and a mother. I understand her struggle. But in my heart, I really valued the fruit of homeschooling for that season, more than solitude. So I persevered, even when my flesh wanted reprieve. I really *was* doing what I most wanted to do, and that changed how I looked at my will. It no longer just rested on the strength of willpower, or the age-old, ever-present struggle between the flesh and the spirit.

Seeing my motivation as the root of my will helped me see two new things. First, it helped me see my own sin in a new way. We cannot examine our motivations in life honestly without ramming right into our own sin, for we are a sinful people. As it says in the Westminster Confession of Faith, we will good *and* evil, with our will only doing good alone when we get to heaven.

> When God converts a sinner, and translates him into the state of grace, He freeth him from his natural bondage under sin; and, by His grace alone, enables him freely to will and to do that which is spiritually good, yet so, as that by reason of his remaining corruption, he doth not perfectly, nor only, will that which is good, but doth also will that which is evil.[9]

We cannot look at the motives of our will without seeing our own selfishness. Dr. Lawrence Crabb, author of *Effective Biblical Counseling*, addresses this issue. He has observed in his years of counseling "that the usual objective so passionately desired is fundamentally self-centered: 'I want to feel good' or 'I want to be happy.'" He continues, "An obsessive preoccupation with 'my happiness,' however, often obscures our understanding of the biblical route to deep, abiding joy."[10] It also obscures and hinders our ability to make our wills, our choices, align with God's.

Yet as painful as it is to recognize our own selfishness, to come smack dab against the glass of our ugly sin like a bug on a windshield, it's necessary and for our good. Such awareness should lead us to repentance. Instead of using Paul's confession of his struggle of doing that which he hates as an excuse for sin, we can repent of the selfishness of our motives when we become aware of them. This sanctification process, this confession of sin and effort to conform to the image of Jesus, is our goal. Because we do what we most want to do, the more sanctified we are, the less we sin.

The second beneficial reason for seeing my motivation as the driving force of my will is that I've been able to use it as a touchstone of my beliefs. As I said earlier regarding the emotions, we act according to what we believe. What we believe determines what we do, and what we do determines what we feel. It's far easier to act our way into a feeling than it is to feel our way into an action. When I exercise my will, it is based on my motivating belief that moment, the belief that is driving me to action. For example, if I choose to eat as many healthy foods as possible when my animal appetite desires decadence instead, I do so not only because it's really what I most want to do, but also because I *believe* that it is the best thing for me. If I choose to study my Bible instead of reading fashion magazines, I do so because I believe that the Bible is good for correction, reproof, and training in righteousness.

You may object to this premise on the grounds that most of us have done things we don't believe are right. For example, we lie or covet when our overarching belief system dictates that lying and coveting are wrong. However, our motivating belief at the moment we lie is what propels our lie—we believe that action is worth the cost. A person who engages in immorality may have a basic belief system that says immorality is wrong, but at the moment of their action they believe the cost is worth the risk. This is a complicated topic, and a deeper discussion of it is beyond the scope of this chapter. My point here is that our motivation is the driving force of our will and it is connected to what we believe.

The power of our will, our ability to choose those things that align with God's will, lies in exercising our faith to believe the things in God's Word. When I must do difficult things, and I succeed, it is because through faith I have believed that this is where God is leading me for a season for my good. Which is actually a very nice definition of surrender.

This is the core of my life philosophy, and it's beautifully seen in these words by Elisabeth Elliot in her book *Keep a Quiet Heart:*

> Purity of heart, said Kierkegaard, is to will one thing. The Son willed only one thing: the will of His Father. That's what He came to earth to do. Nothing else. One whose aim is as pure as that can have a completely quiet heart, knowing what the psalmist knew: "Lord, you have assigned me my portion and my cup, and have made my lot secure" (Ps. 16:5 NIV). I know of no greater simplifier for all of life. Whatever happens is assigned. Does the intellect balk at that? Can we say that there are things which happen to us which do not belong to our lovingly assigned "portion":

("this belongs to it, that does not")? Are some things, then, out of the control of the Almighty?

Every assignment is measured and controlled for my eternal good. As I accept the given portion other options are cancelled. Decisions become much easier, directions clearer, and hence my heart becomes inexpressibly quieter.[11]

It is from this sweet place of surrender that we can say with Paul, "I can do all things through Him who strengthens me" (Phil. 4:13). We can join Jan Karon's characters in the fictional town of Mitford in saying "the prayer that never fails": not my will be done, but thine.

And the will of our Father is always something we can trust. My friends Craig and Coletta Smith took their three-year-old daughter, Rochelle, skiing. She sat at the edge of the chair lift, oblivious to the ease with which her small body could slide right out. "Rochelle," her dad said. "You have no fear." "No," she replied. "I gotta get me some."

Her fearlessness was also displayed when her parents took her rock climbing. I watched a video of her climbing the face of a huge rock that would have terrified me. This tiny girl grabbed miniscule handholds and clung to the rock, secured by ropes and fearless in the safety of her father's care as he climbed right beneath her. As I watched her I thought how I want to be just like that with my heavenly Father. Secure in his strength, knowing that in whatever path he chooses for me, I am safe. *That* is surrender.

In *Girl Meets God*, Lauren Winner tells how a resident advisor at the summer camp she attended in the fourth grade taught her the Lord's Prayer without explaining what each word meant. She wrote:

I didn't know that *will* was a noun, I only knew it as a verb, so my grammatical reading of the second line of the Lord's Prayer—"Thy kingdom come, Thy will be done"—was a little off. I thought "will be done" the verb, so "Thy," the possessive pronoun, must be the subject. And I prayed fervently that *Thy* would be done.

Sometimes in church I think about that still, I think maybe that is what we should be praying for, not just that God's will be done, but that everything that is God's, everything that is His, everything that is Thy, will be done. *Yours be done,* I chant in my head. *Yours Yours Yours. Everything that is Yours.*[12]

I couldn't agree more.

The struggle to live a balanced emotional life and to "conquer" our wills, making them align with God's, is best won in our continual surrender of ourselves, our agendas, our expectations, our fleshly desires, everything, to God. Even when that's difficult to do. Especially then. By faith we can believe that God is working for our good. Our emotions and our wills are woven together with the strands of our surrender, with the threads of our trust in the sovereign Lover of our souls. Yours be done, Lord. All that is yours.

12

To Be or Not to Be . . . Filled

Nourishing the Reservoir of Soul

How well is your soul? If I'd asked how well your body is, or how you are feeling emotionally, you'd immediately understand what I meant, but inquiring about your soul is not nearly as clear, is it? What *is* your soul, anyway?

A common teaching is that the soul is made up of the mind, will, and emotions. In Scripture the word *soul* is used with different meanings and nuances. The Hebrew word for soul is *nephesh;* it occurs 755 times in the Old Testament, meaning mainly "possessing life." I like author and pastor Brent Kinman's working definition of our soul as the part of us that longs for and is conscious of God's presence.

When I ask you how well your soul is, I mean the immaterial part of you, your being, your inner man. Yes, your mind, will, and emotions, but also your essence, the part of you that makes you, you—your truest self. I mean that deep, inward part of you that nobody *really* knows about except you and God, unless you tell them. How *is* this special soul space of your being? Is it nourished, or do you have a soul gone south? Are you living one lifestyle and longing for another? Or perhaps you are so busy that you seldom take time for things that replenish.

To nourish and fill this soul space we need to thoughtfully reflect on *who* we are, *how* we nourish our souls and how to do so without becoming selfish, and *what* we're doing to ensure a well-filled reservoir of soul.

Explore Who You Are

Before we can begin to properly nourish our souls we need to understand who we are on the inside. The great questions that have graced man's mind across history continue today—"Who am I?" "Why am I here?" and "Where am I going?" These topics, fueling the "great conversation" discussed earlier, cover such issues as man's origin, purpose, and destiny, and the answers are important, for they form the foundation of our worldview. But let me offer a few more questions in exploring who we are. Who did God make you to be? What are your natural bents? What things are you passionate about? What longings do you have? What do you love? What renews you, fills you, recharges you, energizes you? Only you can answer these questions.

For me, this has been the topic of countless conversations over coffee or Mexican food with my dear friend Kathy. Like me, she loves to grapple with ideas and reach into that inner part of herself, exposing a piece of it in the

213

comfort and safety of a friend who loves unconditionally. Together we ponder these questions and rejoice in insights. The thinking, discussing, and praying about such things does more than offer coffee-klatch conversation about our own self-indulgent fulfillment. It brings us to conclusions about how to live, about choices we must make, about being a woman in the continual discovery of who we are in Christ and our place and purpose in God's kingdom . . . at least today.

As we answer the questions that explore who we are, we can then act on them to nourish our souls, which is important to our growth, to our wholeness, to our ability to give to others. One question Kathy and I have come back to often over the years is this: What fills your cup? Maybe you know instinctively, or maybe you are not quite sure what fulfills you. Go back to the questions.

- Who did God make you to be?
- What are your natural bents?
- What things are you passionate about?
- What longings do you have?
- What do you love?
- What renews you, fills you, recharges you, energizes you?

Set aside some time to really reflect and pray about these things. Knowing the answers is essential to our being because it affects our purpose and our level of contentment.

The worldly search for answers to "What fills my cup?" seeks an end that is limited to our contentment and self-fulfillment. I don't mean just "What makes you feel good, sister?" That's easy . . . a massage, a pedicure, a great meal that I didn't cook, money in my wallet, and a husband who eloquently expresses that I am a diva he'd die for . . . preferably all on the same day. Yeah, that would fill my cup! But that's not what I really mean. Go beyond that.

What can you do or think about or experience that will nourish the soul part of your inner life in a way that makes you a better person, that recharges and energizes you physically and emotionally, that enables you to serve, that fills you up to overflowing capacity, brimming with readiness to give to others? To be able to nourish your soul, take your questions, your cup-filling ideas, and the exploration of who you are, to Jesus. Ask him for clarity and direction so that your desires for soul nourishment mirror his will for you.

Carving out time to do that enriches our souls and our spirits. Madeleine L'Engle in *Walking on Water* writes, "And then there is time in which to be, simply to be, that time in which God quietly tells us who we are and who he wants us to be. It is then that God can take our emptiness and fill it up with what he wants, and drain away the business with which we inevitably get involved in the dailiness of human living."[1]

What Nourishes Your Soul?

"So what does nourishing my soul look like?" you may wonder. Well, it's as varied as beauty in the faces of women, as different as the sunrise each day, as unique as God made you. Often inspiration comes from others' examples, so while no one but you can answer what fills and feeds your soul (and, of course, you can name several things immediately), here are a few ideas for doing, thinking, and experiencing that can nourish.

What are some things you love to do or have always wanted to do? It might be sports, painting, creative arts, cooking, singing, song writing, playing the cello, ministry activities, or a regular lunch outing with friends. Then there are cerebral cup-filling efforts that are more thought-centered than action-oriented, such as formulating new ideas, exercising creative problem solving, engaging in analytical thinking or the mental creative process. Reading is both action- and thought-oriented. Experiences are also ways to nourish. Some people need moments at the lake or walks in the woods, while others are more fulfilled with trips to amusement parks or the circus. Others thrive on concerts, museums, the ballet, or the experience of listening deeply to a friend.

In *The Garden of the Soul*, Kari Wyatt Kent writes that,

> Likewise, I need to know myself if I am to engage in meaningful celebration. I need to look at what God has done, how he has created me, the passions and loves and gifts he has given me. To live in a way that reflects my uniqueness is actually a way of obediently worshipping God.
>
> My husband, for example, loves tennis and sailing. These things bring him joy. . . . When he takes time for these things, he needn't feel guilty. These things re-create him; they refresh and replenish his soul. They are spiritual activities, and he is, in a way, obeying God by engaging in them.
>
> All of life can be spiritual. If you really love going for walks or doing crafts or going camping, you don't need to feel like those things are not spiritual.[2]

In my own life I instinctively knew many things that were nourishing for me in the inner part of who I am. However, I found greater depth and understanding by journaling answers to the questions above, journaling to God, and asking myself not only *what* I needed, but *how often*. So I'll ask you. What do you need daily in your life? What do you need often? What do you thrive on, if only occasionally?

Understanding what I need and how often has brought great soul fulfillment and growth in my life, especially compared to my youth. Then I was discovering who I was as a person (although that never ends, does it?). And as a new mom I didn't fully understand the need for taking care of my inner self as a means of balancing my caregiving.

These are some things I've learned that I need in order to nourish my soul: Time with God before the troops awake, moments of coffee and quiet before I must interact with people, a walk, and ideally, moments to journal. I try to fit those things in daily. Other cup-fillers for me include learning new things, moments of discovery, reading, time for reflection and thinking, and new ideas, which often lead to another thing that feeds me—writing. I also flourish with laughter, deep discussions, my standing Friday-night date with my husband, and the right balance of solitude and sanguine social times.

And as I mentioned in the chapter on rest, I also need porch time as part of the rhythm of my life, for as John Lubbock said, "Rest is not idleness, and to lie sometimes on the grass under the trees on a summer's day, listening to the murmur of water, or watching the clouds float across the sky, is by no means a waste of time."

Some things require my giving out instead of "taking in," but they energize and fill me as much as receiving things—like exercising my gifts in the body of Christ and reading aloud to my children.

How Do We Nourish Our Souls?

Nourishing our souls takes time. Understanding ourselves and how we tick and praying and reflecting on the matter should result in our planning and making time for those things that will nourish us. Sometimes we need to give ourselves permission to do something for us. We caregivers and nurturers of others' souls sometimes forget that ours are important too, and that the world will not stop if we take a moment for ourselves. Besides, when I do this, I'm a better mother. But doing something for us will happen more often if we plan something to do (or not do) and then make the time in our schedules.

Go ahead and pencil in your calendar, "Get my college watercolors and brushes out of the attic. Buy sketch pad. Tuesday night—paint." Write in your daytime planner, "Put ad in the newspaper to start a reading club or a 'women who think' discussion group." Schedule time to actually begin that novel or start your personal learning journal or go back to school. Give yourself permission to plan and schedule these growth activities into your life. No one else will do it for you.

Another way to nourish the soul is to replenish and restock your mind and heart with images, experiences, smells, ideas, things of beauty, things that foster peace and a tranquil heart. Visit an art museum and absorb the beauty and expressed creativity; sit in the park and soak up the sights, smells, and pleasure of people watching. Proactively fill the reservoir of your soul with that which refreshes you, gives you reason to think or wonder, and is true, honorable, right, pure, lovely, good, excellent, and worthy of praise.

The most important principle of soul nourishment is staying clean before the Father, keeping our sins confessed and our hearts surrendered before God. If we find things that fulfill us but our spirit lives are marred by sins that we do not confess and turn from, we are attempting the impossible. Soul health is spirit health, and soul health requires walking closely with God. We can't expect to fill our cups in the pleasure of painting a masterpiece while we willfully and continually feed our appetite for gossip or judgment or eating disorders. It's like filling a cup with a hole in it; we are never really filled. As we discussed in the last chapter, the will and the emotions must continually be surrendered to God, and in that place of ongoing surrender we also find that our souls are nourished.

We can also live soul-nourishing lives when we use our God-given gifts. Long-term service in areas outside of our gifts, while having gifts we don't use, can lead to burnout and cynicism. Long-term service is better rendered and received when it is within the areas of our gifts, talents, interests, skills, and God's leading. As Paul describes in the New Testament, we are not all called to be hands or feet; we each have specific roles in the body of Christ. Understanding your spiritual gifts is crucial to being effective, especially over a long period of time. Serving and giving to others in areas and ways that match their needs with your strengths can nourish your soul as you nourish others.

Nourishing Our Souls without Becoming Selfish Pigs

One danger of self-help, self-improvement thinking is that it makes it so easy to become self-focused. Susan Schaeffer Macaulay, the daughter of Francis Schaeffer, wrote a book for high school and college students called *How to Be Your Own Selfish Pig: And Other Ways You've Been Brainwashed*. The book is a great worldview discussion for young people, but adults need the heads-up about selfishness as well. A self-focus is easy because man's nature is depraved. I mean, think about it, which is more knee-jerk appealing—swabbing your sick friend's toilets or having that pedicure day, topped off with a bowl of Häagen-Dazs?

There is a way to avoid becoming a "selfish pig" while engaging in healthy, enriching, feeding soul work that increases our capacity and enables us to give more. The secret is to carefully balance soul feeding with heaping platters of some of the basic virtues of our Christian faith: humility, Christlike selflessness, an others-focused world-view, and a heart that is impassioned to glorify God.

We can work at growing in our souls as long as we maintain the attitude of selflessness that Jesus lived and Paul describes in Philippians 2. Working within our gifting *is* soul nourishing, but sometimes we can best attain selflessness through personal sacrifice. It's easy to say, "Well, Paula, I'd just love to help you out in the church nursery this summer, but that's just not my gifting. And no, frankly, kitchen duty isn't exactly it either." I wonder how many people have written in their journals that they feel called to change the dirty diapers of friends' and strangers' children or to scrub dirty pots? If we only do the things we love and are good at, where is the sacrifice?

But, of course, we don't live in a society that values sacrifice; sacrificial living is culturally rare. Susan Schaeffer Macaulay writes,

> Society tells us that we will lose our dignity if we put other people first. One good example is the current attitude that you are being "used" if you sacrifice for or serve others. Be sure not to do the dishes if it's not your turn! If the other person comes back from a hard day feeling grumpy, don't let him flop down while you get his meal and think of ways to make his life easier.

220

Society and culture tell you that you are meant to be a kind of self-serving pleasure machine. Your highest goal is happiness for yourself. . . . Of course, both my mother and I saw this teaching not just as ideas that were wrong. We had also known lots of people who had tried living like this, and who had experienced unhappiness as a result.[3]

Sacrificial living, however, is beautiful. It is an element of a faithful heart and life that God desires, so ask yourself what you can do for someone else today.

Another way to nourish our souls without becoming selfish is to remember that sometimes God chooses to keep us outside of our comfort zones. Operating in an area that stretches us can be an act of obedience. It can lead to growth and become an avenue in which we receive.

One woman wrote in *A Mother's World* about her experience working in Mother Teresa's Calcutta orphanage, where she fed and played with malnourished, parentless children in India's poverty and sweltering humidity. She says,

> Sister Dolores, the Volunteer Coordinator . . . heard my concerns. The cloth draped over her head framed clear, dark eyes. "The Mother says that if the volunteers gain more than they give, that is fine," she explained in lilting, formal English. "It is beneficial simply to be a witness to the work, even for a single day. Then you can use it in your own home, can you not?"
>
> She waited for me to answer.
>
> "Yes," I said. It felt like a commitment.
>
> "There is nothing wrong with gaining spiritually because this kind of gaining does not take from other people—but wants to give even more."[4]

Two seasons of operating outside my comfort zone and living the antithesis of a cup-filling existence stand out in my memory. One was the summer I lived in Hawaii. I was on a summer-long college mission trip, living on Diamond Head and getting great grief from friends back home who teased me about wanting a similar assignment to "suffer for Jesus." There I was, in the land of pristine beaches and fresh pineapple. And yes, there was even a Tom Selleck sighting at the Honolulu Yacht Club. (Hey, it was the early eighties, and it was rather exciting to suddenly see *Magnum* emerge from the sea, walk by us all Poseidon-like, and give us a Hollywood smile! When he spoke to us, we forgot all about giving him a copy of the Four Spiritual Laws tract.)

Nevertheless, it was a summer that tested my faith. We worked full-time jobs during the day and did evangelism and outreach activities on the weekends and some evenings. It was my almost-anything-for-a-buck summer. I was a broadcasting major, so I tried to get a job in a radio station or something similar that would allow me to serve the Lord and fill my cup at the same time. But God had another idea. I ended up standing on pavement for eight hours at a stretch shucking oysters, digging out pearls for tourists. After that I handed out suntan lotion samples in a store, and then I cleaned the house of a man who had been divorced for two years and hadn't cleaned his house since the day his wife left. I was beginning to get the contrast between living in paradise and working in purgatory. God was teaching me humility, among other things.

I finally landed an office job at an upscale travel agency. While I didn't have my hands in oyster flesh or unmentionable aspects of house grime, the new challenge I faced was loneliness. I was usually the only one there all day, which was tough for my social self. So I began to go to work before my shift started, look out the window at the beautiful Hawaiian mountains, and spend time with God praying, praising, and worshiping alone. God taught me about his power to fill my soul in ways that external things, even good things, could never do.

Another time after college, I worked as a city hall reporter in a big city where most of my vastly experienced colleagues had been in the business longer than I'd been alive. I was working in a field I loved but was intimidated and out of my comfort zone. I dreaded going to work. Yet now, years later, I can say I'm glad that God placed me there for a time. I learned professional skills, but mostly I learned fortitude.

The point is that even while experiencing the hard things, we can still grow. Often we grow *because* of the hard things we are called to do. When we are not doing what we love, God often expands our capacity in ways we couldn't have contrived. Soul growth is sometimes found when and where we least expect it, and a surrendered, obedient heart to whatever God brings is what we must bring to him. That's often easier said than done, but it's worth every effort.

What about You?

What are you doing now to fill the reservoir of your soul? Are you plodding along or flying by the seat of your pants to keep up with the pace of life and neglecting the inner part of you? It is satisfying and eternally significant to live your life serving others, pouring yourself into the lives of those you love, but do not ignore who you are in the process. I encourage you to figure out what fills your cup and make time for it in your life. Then offer the non-

223

fulfilling things in your life to God in surrender to his soul work. When we nourish our souls we will find that it is really God, the author and source of all creativity, who is filling that deep space within.

13

I'll Only Go South
If It's Aruba

Why Growing Is Worth It

Of all the possible lovely activities to engage in, there's nothing I like better than laying on a warm beach, shaded by a big umbrella, reading yet another book. Unless it's laying under a beach umbrella, reading, and eating chips and fresh guacamole, with a water bottle and an occasional ice-cold Coke by my side. I'm hoping God lets me do this from time to time in eternity, amidst all our reigning and ruling. With or without the chips. But for now, I'm content with an occasional getaway south of the border. Perhaps someday I might even be able to visit Aruba, which I can assure you is the only way I want to go south.

There are so many ways we can go south as women. Sometimes it feels like our lives have gone south through

no fault of our own; tragedy strikes or horrendous circumstances bombard us. We survive these things by clinging to
our strong faith as if our lives depended on it—because they
do, and also on the love and practical help of people in our
lives. Yet the kind of south I've been discussing is when *we*
have gone south personally, through choices we've made or
apathy about our choices. I'm resolved that the way to avoid
going south in this way is to grow. Growth is the antithesis
of going south. It is accomplished in our lives through God's
power and working, but we are not to sit by as passive specta-
tors in the process. Growth requires change, internally and
externally, and it requires effort on our part. Both change and
effort are intimidating to some. I recently heard someone say,
"I hate change. Why would I want to change?" My immediate
thought is, *Why in the world would I want to stay the same?*

Personal Growth Benefits

To think that this is as good as it gets, that this is as good
as *I* get, is not acceptable to me. This would mean my current
level of everything would stay the same—what I know, what
I say, what I write, how I think, how I love, how I live. That
is a terribly depressing thought. I won't settle for stagnation
and stunted growth. As Gail Sheehy said, if we don't change,
we don't grow, and if we don't grow, we aren't really living. I
know that Jesus doesn't want me walking around not really
living, because he told me he came that I might have life
abundantly! And that means a life that includes change for
the better. If one of our ultimate purposes on this planet is
to become more like Christ, which it is, then this is simply
not possible without change.

Change is nothing to fear, and it's everything to hope for!
The difference between those two points of view is our mind-
set, or what we *think* about change. King Whitney Jr. says that

226

change has a considerable impact on the human mind. "To the fearful it is threatening because it means that things may get worse. To the hopeful it is encouraging because things may get better. To the confident it is inspiring because the challenge exists to make things better." I'm both encouraged and challenged by the prospect of things getting better through change, that *I* can get better. It's not unsettling, it's exciting; the result of the process and the effort is growth. I want so much more than just a fulfilled life, I want to get better from within, to grow more into the likeness of Christ.

There are other personal benefits of growing as a woman. When I grow in the spirit part of my self, I also gain wisdom, knowledge, and understanding, as Proverbs teaches. Each little inch I gain in the battle against selfishness is ground won in compassion and empathy for others. Scripture promises that spiritual fruit is the natural result of spiritual growth—love, joy, peace, patience, kindness, goodness, faithfulness, gentleness, and self-control (Gal. 5:22). My sin nature wars with those things daily, yet the growth and increase God brings in this fruit and the desire for even more overflowing bushels of it spur me on to relentlessly pursue a life that is lived as spiritually alive as my body is physically alive. Spiritual growth is the control center of the rest of our being—health and growth in this part of our inner man, based on truths from God's Word, affect our mind, will, emotions, behavior, beliefs, and wholeness.

As I wrote in part 1 of this book, a life lived wildly alive in spirit is one that can grow with a purpose, can grow from a feeling of emptiness, can be quenched in desert times, and can increase in capacity.

Growth in the practical areas of our physical bodies brings health, vitality, energy, strength, nurturance, refreshment, and beauty. It's an indispensable cog in the wheel of our entire being, and we are no more able to ignore the body and expect growth in spirit and soul than we are able to put peanut butter and jelly together without bread and expect a sandwich.

When we grow in the region of our souls, we add spark and color, richness and depth to our lives. Expanding our minds, handling our emotions, surrendering our wills, and nourishing the reservoir of our souls are ways to grow that bring contentment, fulfillment, interest, and purpose.

Positive, Powerful Influence

If Mama goes south, we can take our children with us because of the impact of our influence in their lives. Consequently, if we are actively growing, we can impact them positively in powerful ways. And if you are unmarried or married without children, you too have tremendous impact as a woman. Everyone with whom you relate, whether in lifelong relationships or momentary connections, is somehow touched simply by coming in contact with you. It may be fleeting, such as a pleasant interchange with a clerk, or it may be life-changing, like a mentoring relationship or the iron sharpening iron impact of a close friendship.

Now, I know this comment will inflame feminists, but I believe that in the biblical worldview, God has given men the gift and responsibility of authority, and women the gift and responsibility of influence. While women certainly operate in various positions of authority (over their children, in jobs, in ministry, etc.) and men are obviously able to influence, I believe we can find great joy, blessing, and impact when we understand the beauty of these God-given gifts and try not to confuse the two. As women, in whatever sphere we live, we are blessed with the gift of influence.

When we grow in spirit, our children or those around us are blessed with the spiritual fruit in our lives that touches them and the powerful impact of a life worth modeling.

Growth in our physical aspects and the regions of our souls can inspire those around us to grow as well. Such growth is multidimensional—we impact others in the here-and-now of daily living, we leave a legacy for those left after us, and we can impact in ways that matter eternally, the most worthwhile reason of all.

Countless people have influenced me over the years. My parents modeled what it means to live a Christian life; my friend Brenda has helped me learn to eat healthier; Kathy helps me grow in my soul through her ability to delve into matters of the heart; Sharon and Sue and others challenge my mind in the pursuit of learning; Lael challenges my thinking, always nudging me onward in the quest for a thoughtful life; Susan challenges my faith and spurs leaps in my spiritual growth; and my husband has impacted my growth in innumerable ways. For all of these people God has brought into my life, and the hundreds of others not mentioned, I am beyond grateful. I am changed. My prayer is that in some small way, God might use me to help others grow, as they have helped me. And when I fail them instead of bless them, when—not if—I let others down and influence negatively instead of positively, I pray that I will become aware of this and never forget to ask them and God for forgiveness, even when I'd rather pretend it wasn't so. I pray I don't forget to pick myself up and trudge on in the march toward growth, doing all God calls me to do, being all he calls me to be.

Getting Started on a Personal Growth Makeover

So where do I begin? you may be wondering. Sometimes when I examine the magnitude of the areas in which I can change and grow, it can be downright intimidating. But like the proverbial directions for how to eat an elephant, we just do it one bite at a time.

229

If you want to get started on a personal growth makeover, let me offer a few suggestions:

- Begin with prayer. Ask God to show you in which areas of your life he most wants you to grow at this time.

- In a journal or notebook, write some of your responses, questions, or reactions to any topic discussed in this book that may have touched you in some way or that you'd like to consider further. Thinking through issues with a pen and paper can help us organize our thoughts and analyze facts and feelings, often clarifying the complex or illuminating our desires and God's directives. To help you do this, here's a brief recap of areas in which we can grow, listed in the order they appeared in this book. Put a checkmark next to those areas where you want to grow and jot down any specifics beside each one as they come to you.

__ A bad habit I'd like to stop

__ A good habit I'd like to start

__ A thinking pattern I'd like to change

__ A skill I'd like to acquire or improve

__ A talent I'd like to further develop

__ A specific way in which I'd like to be productive

__ A character trait I'd like to improve

__ An action, attitude, thought, or deed that would make me more like Christ

__ Something I need to prune in my life

__ One way I can practice abiding in Christ

__ Research or reflection on ways I am already a receiver

__ Spiritual disciplines I want to improve (prayer, Bible study, meditation, fasting, service)

__ My devotion to God

__ My worship

__ My capacity perspective: "I'm a one-size-fits-all vessel" or "God can enlarge my capacity"

__ My water intake

__ A fast

__ My eating

__ Nurturing with "kitchen moments"

__ Exercise or physical activity

__ Sleep

__ Stillness

__ A Sabbath

__ Soul rest

__ More time outside (fresh air and sunlight)

__ My appearance

__ My attitudes about beauty

__ My body's maintenance

__ My countenance

__ My attitude about challenging my mind

__ A learning plan for my continued education

__ My memory or brain power

__ Gatekeeping of what I allow to enter my mind

__ My emotions (handled with practical helps, reason, training, or believing God's truths)

__ My will (choices and motives, actions and attitudes checked against my beliefs)

__ Soul nourishment (What fills my cup? Who did God make me to be? What do I long for?)

__ Overflowing in order to give

__ Other areas in which I want to grow

At times, I want to check off *everything* on that list and add more after that. At other times, I look at all the areas where I'd like to see growth, and I get overwhelmed and don't want to check off *anything*. The best step lies between those two extremes. Prayerfully, thoughtfully, begin somewhere and just take it a bite at a time.

- Make your growth goals specific (and measurable, if possible) rather than making broad generalities. For example, don't say, "I'll try to drink more water," but say, "I'm going to the store to buy a water bottle today." Instead of deciding to add stillness to your life, plan on spending fifteen minutes after dinner in the rocker or on the porch. Instead of saying, "I need to improve my spiritual disciplines," say, "I'm going to add twenty minutes of Bible study to my day." Specific steps, taken one at a time, yield greater results than sweeping generalities.
- When choosing areas in which you want to grow, balance your efforts among the three parts of your makeup—your spirit, body, and soul.
- Resist the urge to approach your growth with just "self-help" thinking by attempting to apply only the practical issues. Focus on the *being* as well as the *doing*.

Remember, you are a woman made in the image of God, a woman who is a receiver because of what God has already given and will give you, able to increase your capacity to grow in any area God sees fit, so that you might live an abundant life, overflowing with fruit, ready to give from your overflow and glorify God with your being. So forget going south, unless, of course, it's Aruba!

A Final Note

Anne Lamott wrote about this nagging little writing fear that I understand intimately. It's that one day you finish your piece, lay it on your desk, and before you can get back to your edits and rewrites the next morning, you get hit by a truck. Blam. I imagined my first draft lying there, a bit naked, screaming, "Just wait till she cleans me up!" But of course, then someone actually *reads* this almost-done-but-still-not-fit-to-be-seen work while you're off fighting for your life and decides that you really can't write your way out of a paper bag. Having others read your work before you have edited it is akin to stepping outside partially clothed. I'm not sure which is more frightening. Well, friends, I got hit by that truck.

As Becky wrote in her foreword, days after writing this book I went into the hospital to have a baby and ended up in a coma on life support for two months. I entered the hospital at the end of the summer and finally came home just before Christmas. Mama definitely went south. It's been a long, difficult journey for me and my family, filled with pain, grief, separation, medication, walkers, oxygen, and rehab, and requiring at least a year to fully recover. Yet it's also been a journey like no other, for we have seen a "real time" miracle—a resurrection and restoration of my body when many thought there was no hope. One of my doctors said, "There is no medical reason why she's alive today. She is a miracle at the hand of God."

The irony of what happened to me in light of my book title was not missed. After I woke up and the fog cleared, someone asked me about it, assuming I'd want to change the title, guessing I'd really missed the mark. After all, I went south but my family managed (with incredible help) to keep from doing the same. But there was no way I wanted to change the title.

I stand by everything I wrote in these pages, and here's why. First, it wasn't aimed at women whose lives go south for a time through things beyond their control (i.e., it's kind of hard to "grow" when you're in a coma). It is concerned with when we go south personally through our choices or complacency, and the joy that comes through our growth. Second, I believe what I said about the importance of growth in spirit, body, and soul, and the interconnectedness of it all. Having been through the worst "south" of my life, I can assure you that every shred of good, of growth in my life, spiritually, physically, mentally, and emotionally, was put to the test during my ordeal. It became cushion and comfort, insurance and ability, in getting through my dark days. Spiritually, God was my healer, my sustainer, the rock I clung to in the dark. Physically, I'd entered the hospital very healthy and in good shape, which my doctors said was definitely in my favor. In the region of my soul, I was content; I'd totally trusted God with the decision to have this baby. Enduring crisis as a result did not make me waver in that trust. I suffered but didn't waver.

Lastly, the experience brought out the best in my family. After years of my husband and me pouring into our children, they poured forth fruit like we'd never seen. The influence paid off and was worth every effort. I am incredibly proud of them.

Do I struggle and fail in each area I've named? Of course, ask anyone who knows me. But do I believe in doing all I can to grow in spirit, body, and soul for my sake and the sake of those I influence, even though this Mama went south? You bet I do.

Now, I'd love to share more about the greatest drama of my life, but I'll save that story for next time when I tell you what happened "While Mama Was Sleeping."

Acknowledgments

I am deeply thankful for all of you who helped pick up the pieces of my work "while I was sleeping." (For those who helped pick up the pieces of my life, I am eternally grateful.)

Becky Freeman, what would I do without you, girl? Thank you from the bottom of my heart for coming into my office, diving into my computer to find this manuscript, and getting it sent off when I could not. I will always cherish our writing "gift from the mountains" cloister week, and your love for my children. Thanks to Ruthie Arnold and Marie Prys for editing my work while I was sleeping and to Kristin Kornoelje, my editor once I woke up. Thanks to Chip McGregor, my agent, for your help and for connecting this book with its home, and to Lonnie Hull DuPont and the folks at Revell for your grace, concern, and prayers during a difficult time. Thank you Kathy Groom for your writing helps and for being such an enthusiastic reader and encouraging friend, Sharon Lindsay for your indispensable research assistance, Lael Arrington for your insightful suggestions, and Susan Britton for all that you bring to my work and my life.

A final thank you to my dear children, and to Tim, my love.

Notes

Chapter 1   If Mama Goes South . . .

1. Brenda Hunter, *The Power of Mother Love* (Colorado Springs: Water-brook, 1997), 121–22.

2. Ibid., 245.

3. Ibid., 4.

Chapter 2   How Can I Give When I Have Nothing Left?

1. Andrew Murray, *Waiting on God* (Minneapolis: Bethany, 2001), 16–17.

Chapter 3   What Am I Doing in the Desert?

1. David Wilkerson, *Have You Felt Like Giving Up Lately?* (Grand Rapids: Revell, 1980), 60–61.

2. Francis de Sales, "Introduction to the Devout Life," in Richard Foster, ed., *Devotional Classics* (San Francisco: Harper SanFrancisco, 1993), 26.

3. Ibid., 31.

4. Chuck Colson, "More Doctrine, Not Less," *Christianity Today*, 22 April 2002, 96.

5. St. John of the Cross, "The Dark Night of the Soul," in Richard Foster, ed., *Devotional Classics* (San Francisco: Harper SanFrancisco, 1993), 36.

6. Andy Crouch, "Amplified Versions," *Christianity Today*, 22 April 2002, 86.

7. Andrew Murray, *Waiting on God* (Bloomington, Minn.: Bethany, 2001), 21.

Chapter 4   I Have My Limits, Right?

1. "Motivation," *Runner's World*, March 2002, 28.
2. Vincent Ryan Ruggiero, *The Art of Thinking* (New York: Longman, 1998), 41.

Chapter 5   So How Does My Garden Grow?

1. Bruce Wilkinson, *Secrets of the Vine* (Sisters, Ore.: Multnomah, 2001), 58–59.
2. Ibid., 98.
3. Ibid., 95.
4. John Piper, *Desiring God* (Sisters, Ore.: Multnomah, 1996), 15.

Chapter 6   Chocolate or Nachos and Other Nutritional Quandaries

1. Stormie Omartian, *Greater Health God's Way* (Eugene, Ore.: Harvest House, 1996), 160.
2. Dietrich Bonhoeffer, *The Cost of Discipleship* (New York: Collier Books MacMillan, 1963), 188.
3. Roger Robinson, "Words to Live By," *Runner's World*, Feb. 2002, 28.
4. Dr. Michael D. Jacobson, *The Word on Health* (Chicago: Moody Press, 2000), 32.
5. Ibid., 92.
6. Omartian, *Greater Health God's Way*.
7. Idea from the Biblical Diet Pyramid Worksheet found in *The Word on Health* by Dr. Michael D. Jacobson, 145.

Chapter 7   Did Sleeping Beauty Exercise?

1. Editors of *Runner's World*, *New Guide to Distance Running* (Mountain View, Calif.: World Publications, 1978), 154.
2. Ibid., 151.
3. Ibid., 157.

Chapter 8   Road Weary

1. Stacey S. Padrick, "Working in a Spirit of Rest," *Discipleship Journal*, January/February 2002, 54.
2. Paula Moyer, "6 Hours of Sleep May be Inadequate," June 25, 2002, content.health.msn.com/content/article 1635.53303.
3. Ibid.
4. Research article by William J. Doherty, Ph.D., Family Social Science Department, University of Minnesota. http://puttingfamilyfirst.us/html/research.html.
5. Tim Muehlhoff, "Putting People in Their Place," *Discipleship Journal*, January/February 2002, 55.

6. John Anthony Page, "The Gift of the Sabbath," *Discipleship Journal,* January/February 2002, 34.

7. A.W. Tozer, "Sweet Surrender," *Discipleship Journal,* January/February 2002, 51.

8. Ibid., 49.

9. Omartian, *Greater Health God's Way,* 216.

10. The 1999 Daylighting and Productivity Study by Pacific Gas and Electric as sited at lightforhealth.com/productv.html.

Chapter 9   You Look Maaahvelous

1. Mabel Hale, revised and expanded by Karen Andreola, *Beautiful Girlhood* (Eugene, Ore.: Harvest House, 1993), 124.

2. Ibid.

3. Lou Priolo, *The Heart of Anger* (Amityville, N.Y.: Calvary Press, 1997), 58.

4. Nancy Stafford, *Beauty by the Book* (Sisters, Ore.: Multnomah, 2002), 9.

Chapter 10   Oatmeal or Rocket Science

1. Sue Buchanan, *Duh-votions* (Grand Rapids: Zondervan, 1999), 12.

2. Ibid., 188.

3. Vincent Ryan Ruggiero, *The Art of Thinking: A Guide to Critical and Creative Thought* (New York: Longman, 1998), 2.

4. Ibid., 4.

5. Ibid., 6.

6. Lawrence C. Katz and Manning Rubin, *Keep Your Brain Alive* (New York: Workman Publishing, 1999).

7. Michael J. Gelb, *How to Think Like Leonardo da Vinci* (New York: Delacorte Press, 1998), 5.

8. Ibid., 3.

9. Daniel Golden, "Building a Better Brain" (periodical source unlocated).

10. Ibid.

11. Gelb, *How to Think Like Leonardo da Vinci,* 55.

12. Louise Cowan and Os Guinness, eds., *Invitation to the Classics* (Grand Rapids: Baker Books, 1998), 13.

13. Jean Marie Stine, *Double Your Brain Power* (Englewood Cliffs, N.J.: Prentice Hall, 1997), 108.

14. Clifton Fadiman, quoted in "Any Number Can Play," *Christianity Today,* 22 April 2002, 79.

15. Ibid., 17.

16. Ruggiero, *The Art of Thinking,* 10.

17. Alan Baddeley, *Your Memory* (Garden City Park, N.Y.: Avery Publishing Group, 1993), 277.

18. Ibid., 64–65.

19. Wes Callihan, *A Guide to the Great Books,* 7. (Available through Veritas Press.)

Chapter 11 Disneyland or LaLa Land

1. Daniel Goleman, *Emotional Intelligence* (New York: Bantam Books, 1995), 43.
2. Jean Lush, *Emotional Phases of a Woman's Life* (Tarrytown, N.Y.: Revell, 1987), 27.
3. Ibid.
4. Joni Eareckson Tada and Steven Estes, *When God Weeps* (Grand Rapids: Zondervan, 1997), 67.
5. C. S. Lewis, *The Abolition of Man* (San Francisco: Harper San Francisco, 1974), 55–56.
6. Jean Lush, *Women and Stress* (Grand Rapids: Revell, 1992), 214.
7. Jonathan Edwards, *The Freedom of the Will*, part 1, section 1, online copy.
8. Ibid., section 2.
9. "Of Free Will," in the Westminster Confession of Faith, chapter IX, point IV, online text.
10. Dr. Lawrence Crabb, *Effective Biblical Counseling* (Grand Rapids: Zondervan, 1977), 20.
11. Elisabeth Elliot, *Keep a Quiet Heart* (Ann Arbor, Mich.: Servant Publications, 1995), 18.
12. Lauren F. Winner, *Girl Meets God* (Chapel Hill, N.C.: Algonquin Books of Chapel Hill, 2002), 147–48.

Chapter 12 To Be or Not to Be . . . Filled

1. Madeleine L'Engle, *Walking on Water* (New York: North Point Press, 1995), 170.
2. Keri Wyatt Kent, *The Garden of the Soul* (Downers Grove, Ill.: InterVarsity Press, 2002), 191.
3. Susan Schaeffer Macaulay, *How to Be Your Own Selfish Pig: And Other Ways You've Been Brainwashed* (Colorado Springs: Chariot Victor, 1982), 102.
4. Cherilyn Parsons, "Mother to the World," in Marybeth Bond and Pamela Michael, eds., *A Mother's World* (San Francisco: Traveler's Tales, Inc., 1998), 12.